THE TEACHING FOR SOC

William Ayers—*Series Editor* Theres

Same as It Never Was:
Notes on a Teacher's Return to the Classroom
Gregory Michie

Spectacular Things Happen Along the Way:
Lessons from an Urban Classroom, Second Edition
Brian D. Schultz

Teaching with Conscience in an Imperfect World:
An Invitation
William Ayers

Worth Striking For: Why Education Policy Is Every Teacher's Concern (Lessons from Chicago)
Isabel Nuñez, Gregory Michie, and Pamela Konkol

Being Bad:
My Baby Brother and the School-to-Prison Pipeline
Crystal T. Laura

Fear and Learning in America: Bad Data, Good Teachers, and the Attack on Public Education
John Kuhn

Deep Knowledge: Learning to Teach Science for Understanding and Equity
Douglas B. Larkin

Bad Teacher! How Blaming Teachers Distorts the Bigger Picture
Kevin K. Kumashiro

Crossing Boundaries—
Teaching and Learning with Urban Youth
Valerie Kinloch

The Assault on Public Education: Confronting the Politics of Corporate School Reform
William H. Watkins, Ed.

Pedagogy of the Poor:
Building the Movement to End Poverty
Willie Baptist & Jan Rehmann

Grow Your Own Teachers:
Grassroots Change for Teacher Education
Elizabeth A. Skinner, Maria Teresa Garretón, & Brian D. Schultz, Eds.

Girl Time:
Literacy, Justice, and the School-to-Prison Pipeline
Maisha T. Winn

Holler If You Hear Me: The Education of a Teacher and His Students, Second Edition
Gregory Michie

Controversies in the Classroom: A Radical Teacher Reader
Joseph Entin, Robert C. Rosen, & Leonard Vogt, Eds.

The Seduction of Common Sense: How the Right Has Framed the Debate on America's Schools
Kevin K. Kumashiro

Teach Freedom: Education for Liberation in the African-American Tradition
Charles M. Payne & Carol Sills Strickland, Eds.

Social Studies for Social Justice:
Teaching Strategies for the Elementary Classroom
Rahima C. Wade

Pledging Allegiance:
The Politics of Patriotism in America's Schools
Joel Westheimer, Ed.

See You When We Get There:
Teaching for Change in Urban Schools
Gregory Michie

Echoes of Brown: Youth Documenting and Performing the Legacy of *Brown v. Board of Education*
Michelle Fine

Writing in the Asylum: Student Poets in City Schools
Jennifer McCormick

Teaching the Personal and the Political:
Essays on Hope and Justice
William Ayers

Teaching Science for Social Justice
Angela Calabrese Barton et al.

Putting the Children First:
The Changing Face of Newark's Public Schools
Jonathan G. Silin & Carol Lippman, Eds.

Refusing Racism:
White Allies and the Struggle for Civil Rights
Cynthia Stokes Brown

A School of Our Own: Parents, Power, and Community at the East Harlem Block Schools
Tom Roderick

The White Architects of Black Education:
Ideology and Power in America, 1865–1954
William Watkins

The Public Assault on America's Children:
Poverty, Violence, and Juvenile Injustice
Valerie Polakow, Ed.

Construction Sites: Excavating Race, Class, and Gender Among Urban Youths
Lois Weis & Michelle Fine, Eds.

Walking the Color Line:
The Art and Practice of Anti-Racist Teaching
Mark Perry

A Simple Justice: The Challenge of Small Schools
William Ayers, Michael Klonsky, & Gabrielle H. Lyon, Eds.

Teaching for Social Justice:
A Democracy and Education Reader
William Ayers, Jean Ann Hunt, & Therese Quinn

SAME AS IT NEVER WAS

NOTES ON A TEACHER'S RETURN TO THE CLASSROOM

Gregory Michie

Foreword by Gloria Ladson-Billings

TEACHERS COLLEGE PRESS
TEACHERS COLLEGE | COLUMBIA UNIVERSITY
NEW YORK AND LONDON

Published by Teachers College Press, 1234 Amsterdam Avenue, New York, NY 10027

Library of Congress Cataloging-in-Publication Data is available at loc.gov

ISBN 978-0-8077-6196-0 (paper)

ISBN 978-0-8077-6197-7 (hardcover)

ISBN 978-0-8077-7804-3 (ebook)

Printed on acid-free paper

Manufactured in the United States of America

Contents

Foreword

I met Greg Michie in 1998 before he published his first book, *Holler If You Hear Me* (1999). I was in Chicago speaking to a gathering of educators. After my talk, he approached me with a big stack of papers and asked, "Can you write a blurb for my book?" I didn't know what to say. "Who is this guy? Why is he asking me to write something for him? How does he know me? Why would he think I was the person to do this?" I remember taking the sheath of papers and thinking to myself, "I'm not going to do this!" I had way too many other commitments on my desk. I did not have time to read another manuscript. I certainly did not want to sign on to something written by someone I knew nothing about. I reluctantly took the manuscript and tossed it into the bottom of my backpack.

When I got back home to Madison, Wisconsin, I came across the manuscript in my backpack and started skimming through the pages. I immediately noticed that the foreword was written by Sandra Cisneros, and that took me aback. Here was a favorite author of mine who had taken the time to write the foreword for this book. Perhaps I had been too hasty in thinking I would not write a blurb. When I started reading the manuscript, I was drawn into the narrative and could not put it down. This author was a compelling writer, and he was telling a powerful story. The book became a best seller that eventually went into a second edition (2009), and I was proud to write a blurb for it.

Later, I came to know Greg as he pursued his doctorate at the University of Illinois at Chicago. His committee was comprised of what I affectionately called the "3 Bills"—Bill Ayers, Bill Schubert, and the late

Bill Watkins. I was asked to be an external committee member, and we set up the oral defense in a hotel room during a professional conference. I remember that when I received the first draft of the dissertation and started reading, I thought to myself, "This is another book." I was right. Greg's incredible skill as a writer came through on a well-researched study looking at the work of teachers of color focused on teaching for social justice. That dissertation became *See You When We Get There: Teaching for Change in Urban Schools* (2005). In this volume, *Same as It Never Was: Notes on a Teacher's Return to the Classroom*, Michie tells the story of both leaving the academy and returning to public school teaching.

When I realized that Greg was going to return to the public school classroom I understood how challenging his decision would be. Like many university professors who began careers in K–12 teaching, I too harbored romantic notions of what it might mean to stand before 13-year-olds to try to inspire their thinking and creativity. I imagined aha moments and shrieks of joy when students discovered new information or realized they understood a concept or acquired a new skill. I conveniently forgot the struggles of getting some students to just come to school or stay awake through a social studies class or have basic supplies like pencils, pens, and notebooks. I also forgot the challenge of working with students with academic skill ranges that were as wide and varied as the individuals who sat before me each day.

When I was a graduate student I recall one of my professors chose to spend his sabbatical year teaching government in a nearby high school. He talked about enjoying working with the students but had forgotten that the simple perks available to him as a professor were not afforded to him as a public school teacher. For example, after about a week of teaching, the university professor received a note asking him to erase the blackboard at the end of his teaching hour since other teachers shared the room. Unlike the luxury of the university where custodians regularly cleaned the boards, public school teachers have the responsibility of erasing their boards (or at least designating students to do so).

Michie's volume brings us back to the reality of public school teaching. The truth is, today's teachers do have to confront labor issues that can involve difficulties like strikes that hurt students, families, and teachers. In 2010, teachers in the state of Wisconsin were confronted with an all-out attack on their collective bargaining rights. The Governor not only removed the likelihood that teachers' unions would survive; he also greatly increased their share of health care and retirement contributions. For days on end the capital in Madison, WI, was filled with protestors—sometimes as many as 250,000 people turned out, more than the entire population of the city. These are aspects of teaching for which we cannot plan.

Michie also describes the oppressive nature of the test and assessment culture that has emerged in today's public schools. Somehow administrators, policymakers, and politicians have reified standardized tests as a mechanism for dismissing teachers and claiming that traditional teacher education is useless. We have heard words and phrases like "value-added," "accountability," and "growth scores" used to reduce students to a number or a score. School is no longer about a wide range of experiences that help students wonder, create, and think. No one seems to care about the quality of experiences students have under the aegis of school. If they do not pass the state-mandated tests, then they are of no value. Nothing about this culture of standardized tests values teachers' creativity and intellect. Our students become governed by algorithms (that none of us understand) that determine who succeeds and who fails.

In addition to the bureaucratic concerns Michie identifies for today's teachers, he also reminds us of the context of teaching in urban classrooms. Consider the contrast between his life as a university professor and a public school teacher in a large, urban school district. As a university professor Greg enjoyed a fair amount of autonomy. He did not teach classes back to back, and he could take advantage of a civilized amount of time for lunch hours and the ability to attend to his bodily functions whenever he wanted to. Also, as a university instructor he did not consider the possibility that his students were in danger of being gunned down in their neighborhoods. Homelessness, gangs, immigration issues, violence, and drugs were not major preoccupations for most of Greg's college students. They did not worry that their university classrooms would be closed down. They did not worry that their communities would be gentrified. Perhaps their only worry is that they would be assigned to work in the kind of school community to which Michie willingly chose to return.

The first-person stories of public school teachers are few and far between. Their class loads are filled beyond capacity. Their evenings and weekends are crowded with papers to grade and lessons to plan. Their work is emotionally draining, and even if they could find the time to write about what they do, it would likely be emotionally exhausting, perhaps even traumatic. Michie's ability to straddle the two worlds of university teaching and public school teaching gives the rest of us an opportunity to know them both a little better.

—Gloria Ladson-Billings
University of Wisconsin–Madison

Acknowledgments

Many thanks–

To all my students over the past 7 years for helping me figure out how to be a teacher again. You give me life and hope.

To the adults at my school–teaching colleagues, classroom aides, administrators, office clerks, parent volunteers, lunchroom staff, custodians, and other staff–for the love and commitment and energy you bring to the work.

To Carole Saltz, long-time and recently retired director at Teachers College Press, for emailing every year or so to ask if I'd written anything–even though the answer was always no. This book would have never happened without your patient encouragement. Also, thanks to my school's social worker, Felisa Roman, who kept asking me, "When are you going to write another book?"

To those who read early (or last-minute) versions of chapters and provided insightful feedback or critical fact checking that helped make the book better: my sister, Lynn; my teaching colleagues, Kim Goldbaum and Nancy Ibarra; Mariame Kaba; Jose Alonso; Katie Hogan; and Cassie Cresswell.

To all the folks at Teachers College Press who assisted with this project. Rachel Banks was an essential collaborator throughout, and her comments on the initial draft helped propel me forward. Thanks, too, to Dave Strauss for another great cover design.

To the many friends (and some strangers) who gave money to my recurring fundraising efforts, whether for books for my classroom library, technology for my media class, or to assist a grieving family in need. Special thanks to Wendy Howe, Sandy Ayesh, John Dahl, and my brother, Kirk, for your generous donations.

To those I follow on Twitter—too many to name—whose work and words have pushed my thinking and shaped my teaching over the past 7 years.

To the students whose words or writing or classroom presence illuminates these pages: Lizbeth Alvarez, Beverly Avila, Luis Avila, Citlalli Bahena, Sherylis Ballester, Cristian Betancourt, Leo Betancourt, Marvin Bonilla, Cristian Bonaga, Bryan Bustos, Carlos Cardoza, Adrian Carillo, Joel Dominguez, Stacy Escamilla, Gerardo Espinoza, Cristal Figueroa, Vida Fresnillo, Juan Carlos Garcia, Charlene Gorman, Dago Guel, Charly Guevara, Jackeline Hernandez, Luz Hernandez, Nathan Hernandez, Antonia Jaral, Angel Jimenez, Estela León, Zahieh Lutfi, Frankie Martinez, Leo Martinez, Yadany Martinez, Samuel Mendez, Jose Montoya, David Morales, Nayeli Muñoz, Jose Navarro, Jorge Olea, Abigail Ortiz, Freddy Padilla, Anahi Perez, Glenny Perez, Karina Quiroz, Atzy Rodriguez, Gisele Rodriguez, Ivan Rodriguez, Francisco Romero, Armando Sanchez, Isaiah Santiago, Veronica Serrano, Eddie Tapia, Jonathan Vargas, Claudia Vega, Noemi Villa, Precious Villa, Arlette Villar, and Carlos Yañez.

To my mom and dad—though you appear only briefly in this book, your influence and love are imprinted on every page. You are part of everything I do.

To my stepchildren—Lisa, Alejandra, Maribel, Jorge, and Miguel—I am awed by each of you and the gifts you are bringing to the world.

To my wife, Lisa, who, even when the world is harsh, persists in finding beauty all around. Thank you for your understanding as I spent almost every weekend for the past 9 months sitting in front of a computer screen. I love you.

Finally, this book is dedicated to the memory of educator and activist Sandy Traback, who lived and learned and loved and led in Back of the Yards for nearly a quarter of a century, and to the memory of Leo Betancourt and all the other young people in the neighborhood who lost their lives to violence during these 7 years.

Author's Note

The stories and events depicted in this book took place over six and a half school years, from 2012 to 2018. The setting is a public school on Chicago's south side. Everything you read here is "true" to the extent that any memoiristic work is: It is a partial retelling, representing one person's perspective, and is subject to the typical fallibilities of memory. When possible, I have consulted colleagues and former students to get their takes on the events described or to act as a check on my own imperfect recollections. Any errors in fact are, of course, my own.

I have changed the name of the school, as well as the names of some adults and all students under the age of 18. In a few cases, I disguised specific details to help ensure a person's anonymity.

SAME AS IT NEVER WAS

CHAPTER ONE

Same as It Never Was

The sounds were familiar. The clang of the bell. The squeak of gym shoes shuffling up freshly waxed steps—first floor, then second, then third. The muted chatter, growing louder as it got closer, of 7th and 8th graders on the first day of school.

The sights, too, were familiar. Comfortable even. I knew this school, these halls, these classrooms. I'd taught here for a decade, from 1990 to 1999, and continued volunteering for a couple years after that. Hundreds of kids from this south side Chicago neighborhood, Back of the Yards, had been students of mine during that time. I'd been well known in the community.

But that was then.

Now, as the first group of arriving students rounded the corner on the third floor and headed my way, I was reminded that I wouldn't be able to simply pick up where I'd left off years earlier. Other teachers received warm "hellos," smiles, or at least nods of recognition from the kids. Not me. I got a few curious looks and sideways glances, but most students just walked past me like I was a bulletin board that had been left up too long.

It was a surreal feeling. Kind of like a sci-fi story where the protagonist returns home one day to find that everything looks just as he remembers it—his family, his dog, the couch, the lamp—but no one knows who he is or why he's there.

Of course, it wasn't altogether surprising that I'd feel this way. I knew when I decided to go back to teaching in public schools after 12 years away—much of it spent as a college professor—that things would be different. But that morning, I felt like I'd stepped into an alternate reality.

It wouldn't be the last time.

* * *

The previous spring, I'd begun telling a few friends and university colleagues that I was considering a return to the classroom. Responses ranged from knotted eyebrows to wary smiles.

"Why?"

"Seriously?"

"You ready to be evaluated based on kids' test scores?"

"You know they're threatening to go on strike, right? You want to go through that?"

"I'm not sure there's a place for teachers like you anymore," one friend, still a CPS teacher, told me, citing the crush of standardized testing and other intrusive mandates.

I had plenty doubts of my own.

I'd been asked many times over the years—mostly by my undergraduate students—if I thought I'd ever go back to teaching kids. My answer was always the same: Maybe. And I meant it. Being a public school teacher had been a huge part of my identity, and sometimes I felt a strong urge to reclaim it.

But with each year that went by, I realized I was becoming more and more comfortable with the relative privilege of life as a professor. I could take hour-long lunch breaks! I could go to the bathroom whenever I wanted! I could go to week-long conferences! It was an addictive freedom, and the more I had of it, the less enticing a return to the daily grind of schools sounded. I'd been 27 when I started teaching the first time, but now I was pushing 50. Would I even have the energy for it? Would I still be able to connect with the kids? Could I find ways to challenge the reforms I knew were choking the life out of so many classrooms? I wasn't sure.

Despite my uncertainty about returning, the truth was that I'd never felt fully comfortable or competent as a university faculty member. When I presented at research conferences or sat on dissertation committees,

I often felt like a fraud—a cut-rate actor playing the part of an academic. I had nightmares about being asked to explain the theoretical framework behind my choice of breakfast cereals. I enjoyed the challenge of working with new and prospective teachers, and I did my best to help guide them on their teaching journeys. But I could never shake the nagging sensation that I was an imposter who would soon be found out.

Beyond that, I also began to question what sort of difference I was making as a teacher of teachers and writer of articles about education. I believed it was important work, and I knew that education scholars could be vital voices in the public dialogue about policy and practice in U.S. schools. Still, as No Child Left Behind morphed into Race to the Top, and as corporate reform efforts flooded districts around the country, I felt increasingly distant from the real damage that was being done to public schools. The waters were rising, and I wasn't even close enough to help stack sandbags.

That April, I got a call out of the blue from the principal at Quincy, my old school. She said she had a few open teaching positions and asked me to spread the word to the soon-to-be-graduates at my university. I said I would.

"You wouldn't be interested in coming back, would you?" she asked with a laugh.

The stars, it seemed, were aligning. If I didn't make the jump now, I told myself, I might never do it.

* * *

A few months later as I drove through Back of the Yards, my new Chicago Public Schools ID in my pocket, I felt, in a way, like I was coming home. The propulsive bustle of pickup basketball games at Davis Square Park. Kids hailing a passing *paletero*. The tightly packed two-flats and three-flats, most of them built during the heyday of the Union Stockyards. A family gathered on their front stoop. Moms pushing baby carriages. A group of young men watching the block for cops or intruders from the other side. It felt good to be back.

But I wasn't coming home. Not exactly. I'd never lived in Back of the Yards, and that distinction was important. Although I may have been considered an honorary insider by some during the years I'd taught here, I'd always been part outsider, too. I was White, for one thing. Though the neighborhood had originally been a port of entry for Lithuanian, Polish, Irish, and other European immigrants, those days were long gone. Now, more than 60% of the community's residents were Latinx and nearly a quarter were Black. Whites were a dwindling minority. The quadrant of the neighborhood where Quincy is located was almost exclusively Mexican American.

I was an outsider, too, in that I didn't have to contend with the daily challenges that many families in Back of the Yards faced. I didn't work a low-wage job or need a second one to make ends meet. I didn't have to worry about how my immigration status might limit my freedom. Police didn't view me with suspicion or frisk me for no reason. I spent a lot of time in the hood, but at the end of the day I drove home. Home was close–in the city, on the south side–but it was still someplace else.

Still, even though I didn't live in Back of the Yards, I had great affection for the community. I relished the relationships I'd formed there. It is a neighborhood of workers and dreamers, of backyard peach trees and sidewalk memorials, of taquerias and mural-splashed walls, of hard realities and boundless beauty. It's a place with a long history of struggles for justice–where stockyard workers united to strike for better conditions, where Black laborers fought to be included in those unions, where Mexican immigrants were met with White flight as they made claim to the so-called American dream.

Much of the neighborhood's beauty, though, is lost on outsiders–and on the mainstream media, when they even bother to pay attention. A web search for "Back of the Yards" paints a grim picture: Two police officers standing behind crime scene tape. A family photo of a teen who was killed. Candles held aloft at a community vigil. A pair of grisly headlines–"Deadly shooting near church" and "16-year-old shot to death."

Despite the assailing gaze of others, people who live in Back of the Yards, or were raised there, know that isn't the whole story. Former students I talk to, most of whom are now in their thirties, speak fondly of growing up in the neighborhood. They are clear-eyed about its challenges but, almost to a person, they say it made them stronger, more resilient. Some still live there, and even those who don't profess a resonant love for the place. That's what I see and feel most in Back of the Yards, as in so many Chicago neighborhoods that have been forsaken by their city's elected leaders: love—fierce and deep and undying.

Love.

* * *

When I finally made the decision to return to Quincy, I thought I knew what I was getting myself into. True, I hadn't had a classroom of my own in over a decade, but I'd spent countless hours in other people's classrooms during that time. I knew that teachers were under intense pressure to raise scores, and that—thanks to a new Illinois law—my "performance rating" would be tied to standardized test results. I knew that the district was scrambling to align everything, perhaps even the daily lunch menu, to the Common Core State Standards. I knew that I'd probably hear far less in the coming year about democracy or equity or justice than I would about current buzzwords like "text complexity," "accountable talk," and "close reading."

But even though I understood all this going in, experiencing it from the ground-level perspective of a teacher was still jarring. At our school's first faculty meeting, we spent an entire session doing "deep dives" into test score results from the previous year, comparing our school's "growth" numbers to those of other schools in our network. As each PowerPoint bar graph blurred into the next, I struggled to stay focused. This isn't what I came back to do, I thought to myself. I couldn't remember the word "data" even being mentioned during my previous tenure as a teacher. Now, it was the centerpiece of discussion, the tail that wagged the dog.

And the tail wagged often. Chicago Public Schools' color-coded Assessment Calendar designated 23 weeks of the school year as testing windows of one kind or another. (The fact that a calendar dedicated solely to assessments even existed was, in itself, a sign of the times.) My 8th graders were slated to take the NWEA/MAP test (three times), as well as the ISAT, the EXPLORE, the NAEP, district-mandated performance tasks (twice), and, for English language learners, the ACCESS.

Even kindergartners and 1st graders weren't exempt: They would sit through two 40-question, "computer-adaptive" exams. It's no coincidence, I thought, that the verb "administer" is used to accompany both harsh punishments and standardized tests.

Along with the accumulating mound of tests, a new mindset had spread through Chicago schools like a contagion. The district's "chief executive officer" called the shots, while "area chiefs" kept a closer eye on what was happening in individual buildings. Emails and staff meetings were littered with jargon from the business world. What used to be merely important was now an "action item." Administrators were on the lookout for "quick wins" in their schools. Hiring was done by the "talent office." If all this were simply a shift in terminology, it might've just been mildly annoying. But the irksome words and phrases signaled a new reality in the city's schools: a business-minded approach, with "data-driven" accountability as its hallmark.

Despite all this, most teachers I worked with did their best not to be consumed or ensnared by the focus on testing and the web of demands that accompanied it. But I could tell that, for some veterans, the narrowed focus of the past decade had taken a toll. One teacher who'd taught in CPS for over 30 years told me he could easily see himself putting in another 4 or 5 years if not for the stifling constraints from above. As it was, he said, he'd probably take an early retirement. "I still love teaching when I close my door and I'm with my kids," he said. "I have a great group—I always have a great group. But all this other junk they put on us? They've taken the joy out of it."

It wasn't only seasoned teachers who felt that way. "I'm overwhelmed," a young colleague told me during a quick hallway conversation. "Really overwhelmed. I have a to-do list, and no matter how many things I check off, it keeps getting longer. And so much of our time is taken up by testing, because it's all one-on-one. Sometimes I feel like I'm an assessor, not a teacher. I keep thinking about all these things I learned in my undergrad classes that I thought I'd be able to do with the kids. But I'm not doing most of them. It's frustrating."

This, I began to see, was one of the real differences in how it felt to be a teacher in the 2010s as opposed to the 1990s. Not that moments of excitement, wonder, and genuine engagement didn't still occur in classrooms—they did. But clouds loomed overhead. People who'd dedicated their lives to teaching and to their students felt overburdened, dispirited, and disregarded.

As for me, I was doing my best to play catch-up—to get to know students' names, bond with new colleagues, teach my classes, create units, attend meetings, set up technology, and reacclimate to getting up at 5 a.m. every morning. Teaching was, in that sense, much as I'd remembered it—exhilarating and draining all at once. I'd recently joined Twitter to keep up with the latest news about the possible teachers' strike, and one of my tweets from the end of week one says it well: "Back to the classroom after 12 years. What hasn't changed? Exhausted on a Friday night."

In truth, I think I was exhausted by Wednesday night. I was just too tired to tweet.

CHAPTER TWO

A Strike of Choices

I had been back in the classroom exactly 4 days when the word came: We were going on strike. I hadn't even had time to get my bearings and, just like that, the ground was again shifting beneath me. I don't think many teachers ever really want to strike, and I, for one, had been hoping the two sides would reach a deal. But when that didn't happen, I pulled on my red shirt and was ready to walk, or march, or rally, or whatever we decided to do. Good thing, too. If I hadn't been, my friend and Quincy colleague, Kim Goldbaum, would have probably yanked me out onto the picket line.

Kim was one of the people who convinced me to make the leap when I was on the fence about coming back to the classroom. A Black socialist and a tireless union activist, she understands the politics of schooling as well as anybody I know. She also loves a good laugh, and students often leave her classroom with a sticker on their forehead and a smile on their face. When it comes to labor organizing and protecting workers' rights, though, she's dead serious.

In the 1970s and 1980s, before I'd come to Chicago, teacher strikes—or at least the threat of them—were a semiregular occurrence. But the next 2 decades had been a time of relatively peaceful coexistence between the Chicago Teachers Union (CTU) and the city. When the strike was called on September 10, 2012, after a year of failed contract negotiations, it was the first time the city's teachers had walked out in 25 years. Chicago's mayor, Rahm Emanuel, wasn't happy about it.

Emanuel immediately ramped up his months-long media offensive in an attempt to turn public opinion against teachers, our union, and our bold and magnetic leader, Karen Lewis. "This is not a strike I wanted," Emanuel said after the action was announced. "It was a strike of choice. . . . it's unnecessary, it's avoidable, and it's wrong."[1]

A strike of choice? Emanuel's implication was clear and targeted to hit us where it hurt: Teachers were being selfish. Our "choice," according to him, was to prioritize our own needs and interests over those of our students.

But it wasn't a strike of choice. It was a strike of choices. After all, it's rare that anything is chosen in a vacuum. Choices are made within a context, a climate, and often in response to other choices made at an earlier time. To call what happened a "strike of choice" was to deny how we'd arrived at that point, to conveniently ignore the prelude of choices that had come before.

When Emanuel's appointed school board rescinded 4% raises due to Chicago teachers according to our contract, that was a choice. When he promised a longer school day without knowing how he'd pay for it or consulting those most affected, that was a choice. When he pushed for a state law that would make it harder for Chicago teachers to strike and require that teacher evaluations be based partly on student test scores, that was a choice. And, when he relentlessly praised charter schools, or backed unproven "reforms" that were widely seen by researchers and educators alike as harmful—those, too, were choices.

All this added up to create a tense, combustible atmosphere surrounding the city's schools. The mayor often blamed teachers, but even with the uncertainty of the looming strike, when it would have been easy to be bitter or distracted, what I saw at Quincy were educators dedicated to their work: upbeat, hopeful, and focused on getting the year off to a positive start with their new classes. "I have a feeling it's going to be a great year," one veteran teacher told me, and others seemed to echo that sentiment with the way they approached their days. Many showed up the week before their paid work year officially began to get their rooms ready. They spent their own money, sometimes hundreds of dollars, on materials for their students or classrooms. And many stayed at school well beyond the final bell, assessing kids' work or preparing for the next day.

So, when Mayor Emanuel called the action a "strike of choice" and implied that teachers were placing our own interests over those of our students, I took it personally. And when the *Chicago Tribune*'s editorial board wrote that the city's striking teachers "abandoned the children they say they're committed to teaching,"[2] I was even angrier. Sure, I'd only been back in the classroom for a week. You could say I was barely a teacher again. But inside, I'd never relinquished that part of my identity. When our picketing began outside Quincy early that Monday morning, Kim with a bullhorn leading the charge, I was chanting alongside all my red-clad colleagues:

> Public education is under attack!
> What do we do? Stand up! Fight back!
> Public education is under attack!
> What do we do? Stand up! Fight back!

* * *

Unlike most of the other teachers at Quincy who had grown up in Chicago or its suburbs, I'd spent my childhood and the early part of my adult years in North Carolina, where unions and union organizing hadn't been a visible part of the social milieu. So, when I started out as a teacher at 27, I hadn't recognized the importance of being part of a workers' collective. I remember wondering why a union fee was taken out of my check every month. Where was the money going? But a few years into my career, a disgruntled coworker reported to the Board of Education that I'd stolen school property. They summoned me for a hearing, and I was relieved to get a call from a union lawyer who said he would be there to represent me. It's embarrassing to admit that my initial appreciation of unions was born out of utter self-interest, but it was an important realization nonetheless: The union had my back.

(For the record, the charges against me were ruled to be unfounded. The "school property" in question was a semioperational cassette recorder that I'd bought years before and had been using in my classroom. Yes, I'd taken it home—*because it was mine.*)

Over time, I came to understand the key role decades of union organizing had played in winning important rights for teachers, along with much improved wages and benefits. In fact, the efforts had been so successful that it was easy for new teachers like me to take these things for granted. Still, I remember feeling that something was missing from the CTU platform in those days. I sometimes felt a disconnect between the issues that were central to me as a teacher and those that were highlighted by the union's leadership. I'd never been able to articulate what I was feeling, though, until I read a piece by Milwaukee teacher Bob Peterson in *Rethinking Schools*[3] that advocated a different model: social justice unionism.

The idea, Peterson explained, was to build on the gains traditional unions had made by moving in a new direction. Specifically, he argued that industrial-style and professional unionism had largely failed to address "key issues of race, equity, and the relationship between schools and broader social concerns."[4] He also gave examples of what doing these things might look like in practice: ongoing antiracism workshops for teachers, recruitment and retention of teachers of color, college prep coursework for students in all schools, youth organizing, and genuine partnerships with parents and communities. This was a vision of teacher unionism I could believe in, but it wasn't one I had seen. That is, until CORE came on the scene.

The Caucus of Rank-and-File Educators, better known as CORE, took over leadership of the CTU in 2010 by winning 60% of the vote of union members. CORE's leadership team pledged that, in addition to fighting for the "bread-and-butter" concerns of the past, they would pay equal attention to bigger-picture issues: contesting school closings, furthering racial and economic justice, promoting culturally relevant curriculum, limiting standardized testing, and more. CORE's platform stood in direct opposition to the business-minded reforms that had swept through school districts in large cities across the country. It was an attempt to bring member-driven, social justice unionism to life in Chicago.

One of the biggest shifts was an effort to convince teachers that "the union" was not a separate entity, above or apart from rank-and-file members, but a true collective where all voices mattered. Early in the year, during a conversation with Kim, I started a sentence with, "But the union should—" and she quickly cut me off.

"Don't say 'the union' should," she told me. "Say *we* should. The union isn't somebody else. The union is you and me. The union is all of us."

It was apparently an old axiom, but I'd never heard it. And it hadn't really occurred to me how the simple semantics Kim pointed out made such a difference. But if this new vision was to mean anything, she was right. We were the union. The union was us.

* * *

As the first week of the strike wore on, the mayor seemed to think public opinion was with him. But it was another sign that he was out of touch. The *Chicago Sun-Times* reported that a survey of 500 registered voters showed that 47% supported the teachers' strike, while 39% opposed it.[5] Out in the neighborhoods, the car-horn vote was even more lopsided. Based on several days of picketing with fellow teachers in Back of the Yards, the honks and hollers of support outnumbered the thumbs-down gestures about 100 to 1. And the encouragement came from a wide cross-section of Chicago's working and middle classes: Latinxs, Blacks, Whites, Asians, parents, former students, Chicago Transit Authority drivers, police officers, firefighters, landscapers, plumbers, streets and sanitation crews, roofers, long haulers, and workers driving tortilla trucks, milk trucks, and beer trucks, too.

The most awe-inspiring shows of solidarity, though, came in the downtown marches and rallies. The sea of red shirts, the common purpose, the swelling pride in the important work teachers do, the reconnections with teacher-friends who worked in far-flung corners of the city. One of my favorite moments was when a large circle of teachers and their supporters formed around a group of drummers and impromptu dancers, all of us bouncing up and down and chanting to the beat, "I believe we are gonna win! I believe we are gonna win!"

And we were right. Seven school days after the strike had begun, a deal was reached, and Karen Lewis declared victory on behalf of the city's 26,000 teachers. "We feel grateful that we have a united union," she said at a press conference. "When a union moves together, amazing things happen."[6] What would become clear in coming months and years was that the strike's impact—and CORE's vision of unionism—reached far beyond Chicago. As Bob Bruno and Steven Ashby write in their book, *A Fight for the Soul of Public Education*, "the CTU reinvigorated a national teachers movement by fighting back. The ripple effects of the 2012 strike are being felt in school districts and union halls across the country."[7]

At that moment, though, they were being felt most strongly in homes across the city. The night the deal was struck, I got a text out of the blue from a former student who'd been following the news. "I like Karen Lewis," he wrote. "She got some gangster in her. She fought a good fight."

That she did. She and 26,000 others.

* * *

We returned to class on a Wednesday. It seemed impossible to simply pick up where I'd left off with my students at the end of week one. I didn't feel right ignoring the strike as if it had never happened.

So, it became our curriculum for those three days. We discussed a *Washington Post* article that gave an overview of some of the key issues that had divided the teachers and the Board of Education. Students asked questions about how the agreement would affect them. We analyzed images from the pickets, marches, and protests. And we broke down the lyrics of a song by hip-hop group Rebel Diaz that had been written in support of the CTU's striking members.

> The union's uprising! Takin' to the streets!
> The workers are united so the Mayor's got beef
> Rahm's a fake pretender with a corporate agenda
> Neo-liberal offender—of course you offend us. . . .
> They don't teach us how to think, they teach us how to test
> They teach us how to work to put money in they checks . . .[8]

It's too easy, of course, to cast the 2012 strike, or any social conflict, in simple terms of good versus bad, winners and losers. But while it wasn't a strike of choice in the sense the mayor intended, it really was a strike about choices–about which direction we the people wanted public education to go. Did we want to keep heading down the same road of more testing, more data slicing, more reforms based on a business model? Or did we want our schools to aspire to something different, something better, something more?

At that moment, it seemed like real change might be possible. Around the country, a new energy was coalescing. In Chicago, grassroots groups of parents and community members like More Than a Score and Raise Your Hand were organizing to question district policies and advocate for students. In Seattle and other cities, the movement to boycott standardized testing was gaining steam. Popular teacher-bloggers like Jose Vilson in New York City were ensuring that the voices of teachers of color were a vital part of the public conversation about education. After years of rising influence in the school reform movement from noneducators and moneyed interests, it felt like the tide might be ever-so-slightly turning.

Thinking back on that time, one particular image sticks with me. A few days into the strike, one of my new teaching colleagues, Saraí Jimenez, a first-year teacher who had grown up in the neighborhood, brought along her younger brother to picket in front of a nearby school. He was 10 years old and in 5th grade. For several hours he stood among us rather unassumingly, listening to the passing cars honk their approval, holding up a hand-lettered sign.

"I am in the middle of a lesson," it read.

Weren't we all.

CHAPTER THREE

Seeing My Students (Again)

After school one afternoon, Myriam, a 7th grader, came to my room to check out a book she'd seen on my shelves. She was an interesting, somewhat mysterious kid—often detached, bordering on unsociable at times, but also big-hearted when confronted with a classmate's pain or a broader injustice. She enjoyed reading fantasy stories and sometimes made colored-pencil illustrations based on creatures she encountered in the books. She'd given me a few of them, and I'd posted them on a wall near the classroom door.

As she was leaving after checking out the book, she stopped and looked up at her drawings. "That's the only place in this school that I feel visible," she said.

Wow. What 7th grader admits that out loud—much less articulates it in those words? I didn't interpret her statement to mean that she felt more visible in my classroom than in others. I took it literally: that the meager rectangle of wall space that held her artwork was the only place in our school where she truly felt seen. Sure, some might shrug off her comment as teenage hyperbole. But it left me thinking for days afterward—not just about her, but about all the other students I needed to make efforts to see more fully.

My first year back at Quincy, that was a priority. I knew I needed to create opportunities within my teaching to get to know the young people in front of me. Even though I was returning to the same neighborhood, the same school, the same grade levels, and the same subject I'd taught before—that didn't mean I knew *these* kids. With over 150 students passing through my room over the course of the year, it would be impossible to get to know them all well. But, as with Myriam, every little glimpse would help.

I knew I would be a different teacher in some respects than I'd been during my first go-round at Quincy. How could I not be? In my years as a professor and teacher educator, I'd spent hundreds of hours in schools across the city, guiding new teachers on the initial steps of their journeys and watching their mentors at work. I'd witnessed lots of inspired teaching and had plenty of time to reflect on my own. But while I hoped all those experiences would give me a revitalized energy as I returned to a classroom of my own, I also wanted to hold onto aspects of my approach that had served me well in the past: a curriculum that took account of students' lives and experiences, lots of project-based learning, regular opportunities for creative expression, and an emphasis on student choice and voice.

So, I was excited to be given the chance to revive the media course I'd created at Quincy in the 1990s. Back then—long before YouTube and Snapchat and Facebook—7th- and 8th-grade students used the medium of video to create narratives based on their experiences, report on community events, and examine issues that concerned them. I pushed to bring the media class back because I knew it could create space in the school day for students to express themselves, to elevate and amplify their voices. A built-in benefit was that, in carving out more opportunities for students to be heard, I would get the chance to get to know them better.

Because media wasn't a required course, it had to be squeezed into the matrix of classes 7th and 8th graders rotated through each day. My teaching schedule that first year ended up being a patchwork of subjects and grade levels: three periods of media with 7th and 8th graders; one period team-teaching 8th-grade reading with a colleague, Nancy Ibarra; and—something I hadn't expected—a period of media with small groups of 5th graders. I'd worked almost exclusively with middle schoolers before, so teaching younger kids would mean rethinking my approach a bit. But that was pretty far down on my list of concerns. What really had my head spinning was the teaching load. As a professor, I'd typically taught three classes per week. Now, I was preparing for five groups of kids each day. For 180 days. And people wonder why so few education professors ever go back to the classroom.

Fortunately, it was difficult to get caught up in being overwhelmed for too long. Kids are good at snapping you back to the present moment in the middle of class, whether with a pressing need ("Can you read this poem I wrote last night?"), a sudden outburst ("Who took my Takis!"), or a side comment that has you laughing on the drive home ("Did anybody ever tell you you look like that dude Mr. Rogers?"). I had missed being in the presence of so many 12- and 13-year-olds, whose senses of humor reveal themselves in strange and wonderful ways. Early in the year, we were playing a genre-identification game when I ruled that a student had miscategorized a television show as being in the history genre. "But isn't everything history?" he argued. "Isn't that sentence I just said history now?"

* * *

A couple months into the year, while scrolling through Twitter, I noticed a few tweets from Chicago teacher and author Kristin Ziemke singing the praises of a website called Wonderopolis. She'd used the site—which answers questions submitted by users, such as "How fast can you zip through the air?" and "Is seven really a lucky number?"—to push her young students to come up with wonderings of their own to explore. Reading her tweets, I was reminded of the "I-search" papers I'd done with my students years earlier, which took the typical teacher-assigned research paper and reframed it as a project wholly guided by each child's specific interests. What I'd loved about that project was how it cracked the traditional curriculum wide open. Rather than having students march lockstep down a path I'd chosen, they pursued topics they found compelling and made choices about their own learning. The "I wonder . . ." idea seemed to have the potential to do the same.

I decided to tackle it with my 5th-grade media class—an eager and inquisitive group. I had them begin by choosing a few pieces to read on the Wonderopolis website, and then generating 5 to 10 "I wonder" questions or statements—things they were eager to investigate on their own. Initially, some had a hard time getting started. "I don't wonder about anything!" Edgar complained. But once they got rolling, their lists grew into fascinating windows into their curiosities, their concerns, and even their lives.

Here are Diego's:

1. I wonder which country had the first woman president and who was she.
2. I wonder who scored the most points in a pro basketball game and what's the story behind it.
3. I wonder if global warming is real.
4. I wonder what it's like in the town in Mexico where my family is from.
5. I wonder why dogs pee on bushes.
6. I wonder how plumbing in a house works.

Some were more weighty than others. But each was intriguing in its own way, each a road worth traveling for a 10-year-old. And almost none of them were questions that any teacher, myself included, would have thought to ask Diego to examine. His classmates' wonderings were equally dazzling and divergent. Ruben settled on the question, "Why did people think the world was going to end this year?" For Fernando, it was, "What was the first video game console and how did it work?" Yuri, who said she wanted to know more about her Mexican heritage, asked, "Why was Pancho Villa so important?" And Adriana wrestled with a topic that was equal parts practical and philosophical: "I wonder why they call it a free country when they have lots of laws that everyone has to follow?" Even the choice of the word *they* in her statement spoke loudly.

The students spent several days researching, taking notes, watching online videos, writing drafts, and deciding which information and ideas were most important to include. To share their learning with others, they created ebooks using an iPad app. Adriana's ebook included everything from quotes about unjust laws from Martin Luther King Jr., to interviews with fellow students and teachers ("Question:

Do you feel less free because of laws?"), to her own thoughts about the limits of liberty in school:

> Another thing about freedom is that schools today are taking our freedom away. In Quincy they are taking our freedom at recess and turning it into something that's not good. For example: they are putting us in groups and sitting us with our class [instead of letting us play].

Adriana's concern with the lack of freedom in schools and society was, in a sense, an implicit endorsement for more projects like "I Wonder." Kids often feel constrained by schooling in all kinds of ways, and the curriculum is no exception. But in the upside-down reality of public schools in the 2010s, where the quest for higher test scores too often rules the day, finding ways for students to authentically direct their learning, even in small doses, may seem like too big a risk for teachers to take. When a teacher feels that her job, her livelihood, is riding on her ability to raise scores, that can easily become the what, the how, and the why of her days.

The "I Wonder" project was a reminder to me that being in a state of wonder—about our work, about the world, and especially about our students—is of crucial importance for teachers as well. Truly seeing a student means going beyond test scores, beyond labels, beyond surface appearances or negative hearsay. It means wondering: Who is this young person? Where is he or she coming from? What animates or silences or worries him? What passions does she have? What wounds? What parts of him or her might I *not* be seeing in the classroom?

The patient pursuit of wonderings like these over the arc of a school year may be the most important part of the work of a teacher.

* * *

Ask a room full of 8th graders at Quincy what they like about their community and you'll get a wide-ranging cascade of answers: the close bonds they feel with neighbors, the *cumbia* rhythms blasting from apartment windows, the summer festivals, the programs at Holy Cross Church, the street vendors, the tacos at Internacional. But if you ask what they don't like about Back of the Yards, a single topic will echo time and again: the shootings.

Gun violence has long been a reality in the neighborhood. The frequency of it tends to ebb and flow, but it never seems to be far from the minds of young people growing up there. A couple weeks before school started that year, a rising 8th grader, Leo, had been shot at close range not far from his family's apartment. Thankfully, he survived, but it was a reminder to all the kids who knew him—and his teachers, too—of how random and sudden such incidents can be. A few weeks into the year, a student scrawled the words "If only we were bulletproof" onto a whiteboard in large, red letters.

It wasn't just in Back of the Yards. Gun violence in a number of Chicago neighborhoods, along with the city's escalating murder rate, had garnered national attention. In an interview on *CBS Evening News* earlier that year, Mayor Rahm Emanuel put the blame squarely on "gangbangers" and their supposed lack of values. "Who raised you?" Emanuel asked, as if speaking to a hypothetical gang member. "How were you raised?"[1] It was a simplistic and bigoted analysis: a slap in the face to parents in gang-plagued areas that completely ignored the root causes of the violence. But what bothered my students even more was the way the deaths of young people in their community were routinely shrugged off by the mainstream media. When a 20-year-old was shot to death that December, online news coverage consisted only of a couple sentences of bare facts: his name, age, the block where he was killed, and the time of death. Students, several of whom knew the victim, wondered out loud why all lives didn't have the same value.

Because the issue of gun violence was so personal to many young people in Back of the Yards, I considered not delving into it that first year. Exploring it in class had the potential to trigger old pain and reopen emotional wounds, and I wasn't sure I'd built up enough trust with the students to navigate that. Besides, the problem and its causes sometimes seemed so vast, so complex, I worried that spending time studying them might just leave us all feeling more overwhelmed and helpless. Wouldn't it be better to close tight the door of the classroom and try to forget about the fear of shootings for 7 hours each day?

It was tempting. But ultimately, I decided that doing so would be like teaching about the solar system while a spreading wildfire raged nearby. Gun violence was important for us to explore *because* it was personal, *because* it literally hit close to home. I believed my 8th graders could benefit not only from looking at the issue and its underlying causes more methodically but also from the opportunity to share their stories and express their feelings about it.

Over the next 3 weeks, we immersed ourselves in the issue from a multitude of perspectives. A guest speaker helped students identify the root causes of gangs and gang-related violence. An online article gave added insight into how guns get from suburban shops to Chicago's streets. Undercover videos showed how loopholes in gun laws made it easy to obtain a weapon without an ID check. A *Chicago Tribune* website that tracked crime statistics by community allowed students to see connections between violent crime and other factors: per capita income, education level, and overcrowded housing. First-person narratives and song lyrics surfaced the emotional trauma that often accompanies gun violence.

For the unit's final project, I wanted to give kids choice in how to express what they'd learned, so I laid out a menu of possible options: videos, written essays, poetry, interviews, and comics. Some students took an analytical route and incorporated important themes and ideas we'd discussed during the unit. Daniel's essay, for example, looked at four potential contributing causes to community violence—segregation, economic inequality, miseducation, and the availability of guns—and proposed strategies to address them. But many of the others—especially those who chose to do poems or comics—were more narrative and personal, with students using their chosen medium to tell stories of how they'd seen gun violence rip at the fabric of community life.

One of the most moving pieces was "How We See Violence," created by Leo, the student who had been shot a couple weeks before the school year began, and Rudy, a friend who had been with him at the time. Both had, at times, been reluctant or unfocused participants in other projects we'd done in media class, but this one garnered their full effort and attention. They interviewed each other, as well as two other 8th-grade boys, and edited together clips with a bare piano soundtrack underneath their voices.

"I lost my friend," Rudy says in the video. "He was 16. He got shot twice—one through the chest, one through the heart. I seen him on the floor, and when the cops were putting him in the body bag, they flipped him over, all bogus." He pauses, never once looking straight into the camera. "I felt bad because I grew up with him. I knew him since I was 3 years old. And . . . it just felt bad. I never thought it would be my last goodbye, like that." Leo, too, remembers the violent death of someone close to him—an older cousin who he says he considered a role model. "I still feel like I'm lost," he says. In the second half of the piece, they recount the day Leo got shot. Leo says that as his leg went numb, all he could think about was his strained relationship with his father and that he might never have a chance to repair it.

Their video mentioned none of the sources or statistics we'd examined together during the unit. They ignored the causes of violence, which was one of the central themes of our study, to focus solely on their own experiences and how they felt about them. In that sense—and this was true for other projects as well—it was less an assessment of their learning than an elegy to lost loved ones and, perhaps, to lost innocence.

Some might consider that a squandering of valuable learning time or say that school is not the place for such raw reflections on fear and loss and regret. But if not in the classroom, where? Where do young people go to process or share such pain and trauma? If schools really care about the social and emotional well-being of our students, our efforts to address them can't be limited to counseling sessions or after-school groups—as useful as those can be. It needs to happen in classrooms, too. And it begins with creating spaces for students to be seen and heard—even when it is painful, even when it is a departure from the district curriculum, even when it can't be easily scored or measured.

* * *

In addition to my media classes, I co-taught one 8th-grade reading class that year with Nancy Ibarra. When the year began, we barely knew each other, so the team-teaching arrangement could have gone downhill fast. Sharing a classroom with another adult can be a two-way disaster if you realize you have conflicting philosophies or commitments or expectations. Fortunately, that turned out not to be the case, and over the course of the year we became good friends.

Every Friday, we had our students write. Writers' Workshop was an approach Nancy had used and developed over several years, so she took the lead and I served mostly as a support. Some days she would have students generate themes for possible writing topics: poverty, hopes and dreams, alcoholism, friendship and betrayal. Other times they would respond to a prompt: Map the block you live on and then write about a specific memory from one of the places. Either way, the message underlying it all was that the students' own experiences were important and meaningful. Their lives, their stories, were worth writing about.

Nancy would often share a piece of her own autobiographical writing as a sort of "mentor text" to get the kids' mental juices flowing. Because she grew up not far from Back of the Yards and was, like most of our students, a child of Mexican immigrants, her pieces often resonated with them on a personal level. I remember students cracking up at her story of wearing an Incredible Hulk costume in 1st grade—purchased last-minute at Walgreens—while all the other girls were outfitted as fairies or princesses for Halloween. Sometimes it was the smallest cultural details that made a connection: "I lived in a neighborhood where I could speak Spanish and everyone would understand me," Nancy read to them. "I could go to the corner and buy *fruta picada* with salt, lime, and chile."

The goal of these writing sessions was for students to draft a collection of "moments" from their lives—short pieces that captured a specific event or time. After accumulating several such "moments," they would choose one to develop into a full-blown narrative, going through several revisions with our guidance. Like the "I Wonder..." ebooks and the final project options for the gun violence unit, the framework of Writers' Workshop put student choice and voice at the center.

And their voices rang out in many tones and registers. Claudia honored her grandmother in her poem, "Abuelita."

I'll always remember you:
Your wrinkled face and hands
Your short white hair
Your maroon colored nails tapping on the nursing home's table
Your sinking sweet smile with no teeth
Your backwards watch
Your last kiss on my right cheek

Marvin wrote about his affection for his pit bull, Zeus:

> I raised him, taught him all the tricks he knows, and I taught him how to be the nicest dog I ever met. He simply loves people and playing with them. If he met you before and hasn't seen you in awhile, he gets super excited when he sees you again . . . You know the saying "A dog is a man's best friend?" Well, it's true. He's my best friend and the best one I'll ever have.

For Lizbeth, the "I am from . . ." poem structure, popularized by *Rethinking Schools*' Linda Christensen,[2] provided a way to put words to some of her sorrows:

I am from a neighborhood where you can hear police sirens every day.
From a place where there aren't enough jobs.
I am from a mom that says "Te calmas o te calmo."
From a mother who cooks really well, and makes the best mole in the whole world . . .
I am from a family that is poor, and when there is no money there's nothing to do.
I am from a brother who is in jail.
In jail not only because of violence in the neighborhood
But because of a father who did not do his job . . .

I am from a life story full of sadness.
From an old pair of shoes and feet that have passed by a lot.

From a soul that has suffered
and when you get to know it, you will cry.

Although the bulk of the content and structure of the writing lessons came from Nancy, I did come up with one good idea toward the end of the year. What if we had each student choose a favorite piece and compile them in a collection? Students could type up their stories, we'd print them out, and then assemble the spiral-bound books together as a class. In the era of texting, YouTube, and social media, it sounded decidedly old-school. But Nancy was enthusiastic about the idea, and so were the students. It became the year's culminating project.

Nancy wrote the introduction for the book, which we titled "Ordinary Lives, Extraordinary Stories." It read, in part:

> We live with the fear of the gun violence in our neighborhood, grief caused by loss of loved ones, challenges which drive some of us a little over the edge. But above all, something always resonates within us and that is hope for our future and love for our families. There's a strong belief among us that there is good in this world, and we are on the path to finding that good.

Each student got two copies of the book to keep. Nancy and I kept the extras for our classroom libraries, and the following year they were checked out just as often as the most popular young adult titles. Within a few years, all the copies had disappeared. Permanently borrowed, I like to think, because of the familiarity, the resonance, the power of the stories inside.

* * *

That should be a happy enough ending, but I can almost hear the objections of the "student achievement" crowd. But where is the rigor? What about the Common Core State Standards? I remember reading that David Coleman, one of the lead architects of the Common Core, famously belittled "personal" writing in schools in a presentation to the New York State Department of Education. "[A]s you grow up in this world you realize people really don't give a shit about what you feel or what you think," Coleman said. "What they instead care about is can you make an argument with evidence."[3]

It was a bombastic and intentionally provocative statement. But it still irked me. Yes, teens need to be able to understand evidence and make convincing arguments. In our reading/writing class, we tried to help them do that as well. But they also need a safe space to sort through their feelings, to find meaning in their experiences. They need to feel seen. They need to be heard. They need to know that they matter.

When teachers fail to create spaces to see students fully, it not only hampers our ability to teach them well. It prevents us from envisioning what they are capable of doing and being, what they might become. In his bestselling book, *Between the World and Me*, Ta-Nehisi Coates recounts his years as a student in Baltimore's public schools, where the curriculum seemed hopelessly disconnected from the life he then knew. "I was a curious boy," Coates writes, "but the schools were not concerned with curiosity. They were concerned with compliance."[4]

Similarly, in their book *To Teach: The Journey, in Comics*, William Ayers and Ryan Alexander-Tanner tell of a retired teacher's recollection of one of her former students, jazz great Ella Fitzgerald, upon the iconic singer's death. "I've thought about it all these years," the woman says. "I had the great Ella Fitzgerald in my class and I didn't even know it."[5] The tragedy, the authors suggest, is that all the kids in the class were Ellas—or Ta-Nehisis—each with unique gifts, a singular story, something of value to offer.

And so it is with all students, in all classrooms.

CHAPTER FOUR

Hellos and Goodbyes

The first day he came into my class, Salvador told me his family would be moving soon.

"How soon?" I asked.

"I dunno. Maybe next week."

The next week came and went, and Salvador was still there. He was a sweet 13-year-old, and he seemed to like my media studies class. He participated in discussions, asked lots of questions, and often lingered afterward to help me straighten up. I noticed early on that he had to squint hard to see the whiteboard from across the room, and I made a mental note to check on getting him some glasses.

"I'm gonna miss this class when I move," he told me a week after he'd first mentioned it.

"Is that still happening?" I asked.

"Yeah. I don't wanna go, but my parents say we gotta."

Whenever he'd bring it up, I'd try to get more details, but Salvador didn't seem to know any. Or if he did, he wasn't sharing. He wasn't sure what neighborhood the family was moving to, how far away it was, what school he'd be going to, or even if he'd still be in Chicago. It was all a mystery. A couple colleagues told me he'd been saying he was going to move since the previous school year. But every time it turned out to be a false alarm.

After a few weeks, I began to wonder if Salvador's "I'm moving" story was just that—a story he told to make sure his teachers noticed him. Maybe he imagined us across a crowded room, without our glasses, squinting to bring him into focus, to see who he really was. Maybe the story was a symbolic wave of the arms that said, "Hey! Don't forget about me!"

Or maybe he just didn't want to vanish from our classrooms unnoticed, which isn't uncommon in city schools. Living in poverty doesn't always afford parents the luxury of planning ahead. I remember occasions when, out of nowhere, the intercom buzzed, a kid was called down to the office without fanfare, as if to retrieve a note, and that was it. Transferred. Gone. Never to be seen or heard from again.

* * *

I heard Veronica before I ever saw her. It was the first week of school, and I was standing at my post outside the boys' washroom, helping to supervise the after-lunch toilet break. At the other end of the hall, a voice, loud and accusatory, cut through the usual rumble of chatter. I don't remember the exact words, but it was something like, "Fuck that bitch! I didn't say nothin' to her lil' ho ass!" Something pretty close to that.

When I looked to see from whose mouth the words had flown, I saw Veronica stomping down the hall, eyes blazing, her ponytail snapping behind her as if to add a few more exclamation points. Students parted like the Red Sea as she came through. She turned a corner and disappeared into a classroom.

"She's trippin'," one of the boys waiting in line for the bathroom said.

"She's always like that," another kid added, then shrugged as if to say, "Glad I don't have to deal with it."

Part of me was thinking the same thing. Veronica wasn't in my class yet—I wouldn't have her until the next quarter. But whether she was in your class or not, her presence was felt throughout the third floor. Unlike Salvador, who could easily go through an entire school day without drawing any attention, Veronica forced teachers to take her into account. "I hate this fuckin' school!" I heard her say more than once. But if she had to be here, she seemed to have decided, it was going to be on her terms.

One morning a few weeks later, I was in my classroom planning during a prep period when I heard Veronica's voice again. As before, she was upset, letting curse words fly, going back and forth with her homeroom teacher who was trying to calm her down. Since I didn't have a class that period, I went out in the hall to see if I could help. I offered to take Veronica to my room for a bit to cool down.

"Do you want to go with Mr. Michie?" her teacher, Ms. Wagner, asked.

Veronica snarled. "Why I wanna go with him? I don't know him."

"Well, you can't stay out in the hall," Ms. Wagner said. "And I have to go back in with the rest of the class."

Reluctantly, Veronica walked back to my room with me. "Don't worry," I told her. "We don't have to have a conversation."

And we didn't. Veronica stewed, arms folded tightly, mumbling under her breath. I pretended to work on a lesson, wondering what she had been through that had left her so hardened, and what it would take to begin to break through her many-layered shell.

* * *

Winter break came and went, and Salvador was still in my class. His moving date kept getting pushed back. "The end of February," he told me. When March came, he said he'd be leaving "after the ISAT test is over." But the following Monday the ISAT was finished and he was still in school. After class the next day, he told me his parents had started moving some of their stuff to a new apartment, but he was still vague on the details and unsure when he'd be transferring.

That Friday, Salvador's class worked on media analysis projects while I met with individual students at a back table. The period had been kind of hectic, and I was frustrated with the lack of focus some students were showing. When I looked up and saw Salvador out of his seat and taking pictures with an iPad instead of working on his assignment, I yelled at him.

"Salvador, what are you doing?" He froze, and other kids' heads turned toward him. "Turn off the iPad! Sit down! Did I say it was time to take pictures?" Salvador, embarrassed that I'd called him out, slunk back to his seat. He didn't stay after class to help clean up.

When the last bell rang at 2:45, I began my usual end-of-the-day routine: shifting piles of papers and books around on my desk, locking cabinets, and checking my email. I heard a knock and looked up to see Salvador standing in the doorway.

"I just wanted to come say goodbye," he said, eyes cast down at the floor. "This was my last day. I start my new school Monday."

What? Even with the months-long buildup to this moment, I somehow felt I'd been blindsided by it. He was leaving now?

I fumbled for something comforting to say, told him we'd miss him, that he'd make new friends, and shared a story of changing schools midyear when I was in 4th grade. I asked if he was feeling sad. He bit his lower lip, looked at his shoes, and nodded.

I felt awful. That I wasn't prepared for this. That I'd never gotten him the glasses he needed. That I'd yelled at him just a few hours earlier. Shit.

If only he'd told me that morning during class, I could've done something. I could've created space for closure with the rest of the group, allotted time for students to wish him well, taken a group photo, passed around a card for them to sign. Something. Instead, despite all the fair warnings he'd provided of his departure, it was passing as unceremoniously as the daily washroom break. Monday would come and Salvador's chair would simply be empty.

It's not that I wanted to make a big production of it. But if creating a welcoming and affirming classroom environment is part of a teacher's job, isn't it also our responsibility to say a decent goodbye?

Maybe I was making something out of nothing. Maybe Salvador was fine with the way things were ending. But I couldn't help thinking that he'd wanted it to be different somehow, and that I'd missed an opportunity to give him a last day he could remember.

* * *

By the time Veronica was in my media class, I'd gotten to know her a little better. She'd used my room as a space to cool down several more times, and I'd learned a few things about how to address her moods and needs. Still, I didn't feel like I was making a lot of headway with her. A wall was still up between us, and she rarely produced any work in class. She was often resistant, combative, and openly dismissive of other students' ideas ("That's some dumb shit right there."). Had it not been for a stroke of wild luck, and the patient relationship-building of another teacher in another school 2 years earlier, I may have never seen another side of her.

But one day when she was staying with me during recess, I asked her about her school experiences before Quincy. Had she ever liked school? Had she ever had a memorable teacher?

"One," she said. "Ferrer. In 6th grade."

Wait a minute. Ferrer? What were the chances? I knew a guy named Fernando Ferrer who I'd met years earlier when he was just starting out as a teacher. We'd kept in touch here and there, but I hadn't talked to him in a while. "Was his first name Fernando?" I asked.

"Wait–you know Ferrer?" Veronica asked.

"I know *a* Ferrer," I said. "Fernando."

"Yeah, that's him–Ferrer," she said excitedly. "Mr. Ferrer. He's a cool-ass teacher." She was smiling. Maybe not quite beaming but by Veronica standards, a pretty big-ass smile.

"You know how to get in touch with him?" she asked.

A few days later, during my prep period, we were on the phone with Fernando. Veronica reminisced about her time in his class. Fernando told her how happy he was to hear from her. He asked lots of questions. He told her she could trust me, that I was a good teacher. He was warm and generous and encouraging–reminding her of her goodness, of what he'd seen in her.

The change in Veronica wasn't instant after that call, and the difference, even as it emerged, wasn't night and day. But Fernando had created an opening, peeled back a couple layers of her protective shell. Gradually, she began tearing away a few on her own. It turned out that much of her anger was really a deep, unhealed hurt: The summer after 6th grade, her family's apartment had caught fire. Everyone had escaped except for her younger brother, Aaron. His death, and the empty space it left behind, haunted Veronica's dreams and her waking life.

My sense was that she didn't know how to process her sadness and pain, so it spilled out as anger and fury—at other kids, at Ms. Wagner, at me, at the world. One day as the rest of the class worked on identifying bias in media pieces, I talked with her about trying to write about Aaron—some memories, or maybe a poem. She resisted at first but eventually got out a pencil and notebook. When she was finished, she said she didn't like it. It didn't sound right, she said. I got out my phone and quickly took a photo of it.

"You're taking a picture of my poem?" Veronica asked. "You're weird."

"In case you lose it," I said.

"You're weird," she repeated.

The poem was raw and needed work, but it was a start. She was getting her feelings on paper, maybe beginning to work through a little of the grief. She left it aside for several days, but a week later, she came into class, threw down her notebook, and said, "Hey—you still got that picture of my poem? I wanna finish it." She had lost her copy.

Over the next couple weeks, she revised the poem several times, typed it up, brought in some photos of Aaron to scan, and used the iPad to create an ebook version. She didn't have a computer at home, so she printed a copy to take to her mom. All the while, the rest of the class was doing completely different assignments, but I thought the poem and ebook were what Veronica needed. She seemed to agree. Weeks after she finished it, she'd occasionally open the iPad, navigate to her ebook, and reread it once more. The same words, her words, over and over, again and again. A healing mantra of her own.

* * *

In the Hollywood version of this story, Veronica would seek me out on graduation day, give me big hug, and tearfully express how much the process of writing the poem had meant to her. We'd take a few photos together, say farewell, and promise to keep in touch. But none of that happened. Her attendance had been sporadic at the end of the year, and we never had a moment to have any closure. I'd hoped to connect with her after the graduation ceremony, but as the students filed out of the gym, their robes and sashes glinting in the sunlight, she waved once and was gone. To this day, I've never seen or heard from her again.

In one of the final scenes in the film version of *The Life of Pi*, the adult Pi Patel says, "I suppose in the end, the whole of life becomes an act of letting go. But what always hurts the most is not taking a moment to say goodbye."[1] Thanks to Salvador knocking on my door on his final day, we did get a moment—a moment I think he needed. But what I realized after the graduation was that, with Veronica, I was the one who needed the goodbye.

The story that's often told about the teacher-student relationship is of the lasting impact teachers make on young people in their classes. Teacher-hero films like *Mr. Holland's Opus, Freedom Writers,* and *Stand and Deliver* come to mind. It's not just a concocted storyline, though. Fernando had clearly made a difference with Veronica when she was a 6th grader, and adults the world over can recall *that teacher*—the one who saw something in them that others did not.

But the reverse is also true. Kids leave indelible impressions on their teachers as well. What we learn from our relationships with certain students can change not only how we teach but how we see, and understand, and act in the world. Sometimes it's the students who confound or challenge us most who leave the biggest mark. And sometimes, too, they are the ones we find ourselves thinking about years later—wondering how they're doing, and hoping that, wherever they are, they feel loved, and healed, and happy.

CHAPTER FIVE

Not Highly Qualified

I should have expected it.

When I agreed to come back to Quincy to teach media, I should have known that it wouldn't last. In a behemoth school system like CPS, with a revolving door of CEOs and budget cuts that recur like bad dreams, there are too many potential complications to be certain that any good thing can survive for long.

In May of my first year back, my principal informed me that our school had lost funding for a teaching position, which would necessitate shuffling assignments for the coming year. My media class would be one of the casualties. I would teach social studies instead.

I was disappointed. Deflated. But I knew better than to feel sorry for myself. Losing the media course was a huge letdown, but thousands of students and teachers across the city's south side were going through a much more traumatic upheaval.

That same month, the Board of Education would vote on a plan by Mayor Rahm Emanuel to close 54 schools—almost all of them in Black communities. The original proposal had been to shutter over 100 buildings, but after months of protests by parents, community activists, students, and teachers, the list had been narrowed to 54. All along, Emanuel pitched the move as a cost-savings measure that was good for kids. "For too long, too many of our children have been trapped in underutilized, under-resourced schools,"[1] he said in the weeks leading up to the vote on the closings. But it was a narrative told strictly in the passive tense, a story missing a crucial set of actors. After all, if the kids had been "trapped" for so long, who'd held them captive? If the schools had been under-resourced, who had failed to provide those resources?

As the vote on the closings drew near, I marched with hundreds of others through several of the targeted south side neighborhoods to contest the proposed actions. Signs of systemic neglect and abandonment were all around: vacant storefronts; overgrown lots; foreclosure notices slapped on front doors of numerous homes; a small, unadorned, and untended playground. It was clear that the children in these communities—almost all of them Black—had been failed in many ways, and for many years, by those in power. None of this, however, seemed to faze the members of the mayor's hand-picked Board of Education, who voted to close 50 of the 54 schools. It was the largest mass shuttering of schools in a single city in U.S. history.[2]

In that context, having the plug pulled on my media class wasn't such a big deal. Still, I'd spent a year building the course from scratch, so it took a couple days for me to shake myself out of the doldrums. But once I did, I tried to get focused on sketching out a social studies curriculum. Then another possible twist was added to the mix. During a conversation with Kim, she proposed that we do a trade for the coming year: I'd take one of her reading classes in exchange for her taking on a section of social studies.

At Quincy, as in many Chicago schools, the class known as "reading" is really English language arts. It encompasses reading, writing, speaking, spelling, grammar, vocabulary, and maybe even origami and minor plumbing repair. Kim taught five sections of it, and the grading was a beast: A single student essay, even if only a couple paragraphs long, could easily take 7 or 8 minutes to read, comment on, and offer suggestions for improvement. Multiply that by 150 students and you're spending 20 hours outside of school grading one assignment. Even for a skilled, veteran teacher like Kim who knows the routine, it's an overwhelming, oppressive workload. Having one less reading class, and 30 fewer essays to grade each time, would at least make a dent in the mountain of papers on her desk.

I was sympathetic and wanted to help, but as I mulled over the swap that night, many of my initial considerations were selfish ones. For one, it would be more work for me over the summer. A second new subject to prepare for, additional research to do, more resources to gather. My sparse classroom library would also need to be beefed up considerably. But more than that, it meant I would no longer be able to fly under the radar as a teacher of a subject that wasn't tested and didn't "count." Since media and social studies had no test scores associated with them, nobody paid them much attention. But for reading and math, the stakes were high. Scores for those subjects largely determined every Chicago school's rating, as well as 8th graders' high school options. As much as I wanted to think I wouldn't let that pressure bother me, I was concerned that it might.

But part of me was also intrigued by the challenge. For years, both in public forums and with my university students, I had railed against the pernicious influence of testing on public school classrooms: the narrowing of the curriculum, the myopic focus on skills, and the blind devotion to chasing scores at the expense of connecting learning to students' lives and experiences. But most of my own teaching had been in nontested subjects, largely out of reach of the long claws of high-stakes accountability. How would I respond when they were grasping at me?

I wasn't sure. But the more I thought about the possibility, the more I was drawn to it. Except for the team-teaching experience with Nancy, I'd taught reading only once before, 15 years earlier. But all these years later, I remembered the thrill—yes, that's the right word, *thrill*—of seeing young people connect to books and poetry in ways that helped them find meaning in their own lives. That's what art does, of course, but when reading is a task or a chore, it rarely happens. When teens discover books that speak to them, though, a profound shift begins to take place. One of my students' favorites back then was an anthology of essays written by New York City teens called *Starting with 'I.'* Word of mouth was so strong from my reading class that even kids in other classes came by to check the book out. Within its pages, they saw and heard themselves.

Small successes like that didn't mean I would be able to do something similar this time around. I still had serious reservations about how it would go. But spurred on by my no-doubt romanticized memories, I decided to take on the reading class.

* * *

I spent lots of time that summer getting prepared. I decided early on that I was going to teach reading the way I believed was best for my students—test scores be damned: a workshop approach with lots of student choice, shelves full of great books, heavy doses of poetry, challenging articles on current issues, and plenty of time for discussion and independent reading. Two books helped fortify my plan: Nancie Atwell's *The Reading Zone*[3] and Donalyn Miller's *The Book Whisperer.*[4] Both were full of practical ideas about how to bring such an approach to life, from setting expectations to managing a classroom library to making space for students to share "book talks" with peers. They also provided constant reminders of a simple idea that schools hell bent on raising test scores seem to forget: Once they've gotten the basics of decoding and phonics figured out, kids become better readers by reading lots of books they love. One of my main roles would be to provide a space and a structure for them to do just that, and to discover, if they hadn't already, what a joyous experience it can be.

To make that happen, I needed more books for teens. Lots of them. I only had about 100 in my classroom collection, and the ones that had been left behind by a previous teacher were mostly fading classics with White protagonists: *The Adventures of Tom Sawyer, Little Women, The Great Gatsby.* Those might have had some appeal had I been teaching in a prep school—or in the 1940s. But for the many reluctant and struggling readers I was likely to encounter, or students who had simply never had the experience of finding a book that spoke to them, they probably wouldn't light the spark. So, I also spent large chunks of time that summer reading online reviews of recent young adult titles and visiting secondhand bookstores, digging through the shelves for novels and comics I thought would pique my students' interest. I put out an online plea to friends and family for donations to help fund the cause, and their generosity helped me accumulate over 250 additional books by the time classes began that fall.

All of this had me excited to get started, but doubts about my approach—or, more accurately, my ability to carry it out—continued to creep in. *What about the tests?* During my first tenure as a teacher in the 1990s, I never would've considered revising my methods based on how I thought it might impact test scores. Kids took the tests; we got the scores. The fate of the planet was not riding on them. But in this new environment, second thoughts dogged me. As much as I believed in the plan I'd laid out, I worried that the results wouldn't show up where it mattered. As the first day approached, I heard whispers in my head that I rarely had before: *But is this really going to raise their reading scores?* I hated to admit it, but it was true.

Also true: I wasn't certified to teach reading—a slight hitch in the plan. I'd taught in Chicago classrooms for 10 years, had a master's and PhD in curriculum and instruction, and had been a professor of education for nearly a decade. Although none of that guaranteed that I would be a good reading teacher, it should have at least let me in the door to give it a try. Yet in the parlance of federal and state education guidelines at the time, I was "not highly qualified" to teach reading. What this meant was that my principal would have to send a letter home to parents announcing that I, their child's reading teacher, was not technically qualified for the job. It was hard to imagine a more inauspicious way to begin.

* * *

One of Nancie Atwell's ideas that stuck with me most was that, to become readers, kids need the time and space to get "in the zone."[5] By this she means the type of reading experience where you are completely immersed in a story, where your chair, the floor beneath you, and even the book you're holding seem to slip away as you are transported to the American South of the 1920s, to the peak of Mount Everest, to Hogwarts or Panem or Wakanda.

Good readers know this experience well, but struggling readers may not, so I began the year by emphasizing the importance of getting in the zone with a book. To help students understand what that meant, I showed them video clips of athletes and dancers and freestyle rappers doing something similar: getting so lost in the moment that the court or dance floor or crowd become a blur, the past and the future momentarily dissolve, and all that exists is the present moment. Watching highlights of Nate Robinson's 23-point fourth-quarter outburst for the Chicago Bulls in a 2013 playoff game seemed to make the point well.

This led directly to my second priority in setting the stage for the year: getting students excited about books. Here again, I borrowed ideas from Atwell and Miller, as well as from amazing people I followed on Twitter, like Brooklyn-based teacher and literacy guru Cornelius Minor. I did book talks about titles I thought might interest certain kids, we watched short video "book trailers" a couple times a week to build excitement, and when we got in a batch of new titles, we did "book walks" around the classroom to give students the opportunity to look at each one, skim the back cover description, and add titles to their "Books to Read" lists.

The independent reading requirements for the class were straightforward: Choose books you want to read, hold yourself accountable, and finish at least three novels per quarter—12 for the year. No book reports or reading logs, which can quickly turn the joy of reading into the drudgery of proving you've done it. Instead, students were tasked with keeping their own simple records of progress on the honor system. I knew other teachers had loftier expectations (Donalyn Miller writes that her students read an average of 40 books per year[6]), but at the time, I thought 12 was ambitious, even risky. Most kids reported that they had read just a few books on their own the previous year, and some hadn't finished any.

"I don't like to read!" Bryan announced the first week of class from the back row—actually just a single desk at the rear of the class where he had chosen to sit. "It's boring."

"Yeah, a lot of people think that when they've never really found a book they love," I said. "You're gonna find one, though. It might just take a little time."

A few other students were also resistant: fidgety during independent reading time in class and often failing to complete their 20 minutes of reading at home each night. But most were starting to discover books they enjoyed, even loved. For Silvia, it was *Monster*, Walter Dean Myers' story of a Black teen writing a screenplay of his own murder trial. For Lisette, it was Meg Medina's *Yaqui Delgado Wants to Kick Your Ass*. Fausto couldn't get enough manga (even when I was trying to teach), Itzel devoured paranormal romance (though she consistently failed to turn in classwork), and Joel, after abandoning book after book, finally got pulled in by Simone Elkeles's *Perfect Chemistry* series. Thirty kids, 30 lives, 30 unique and idiosyncratic readers.

Just as *Starting with 'I'* had done with my students 15 years before, a few titles became word-of-mouth sensations. By November, almost half the class had read *The Barrio Kings*, William Kowalski's tale of a former gang member's efforts to settle down and leave his troubled past behind (recommended to me by Cornelius Minor). It is what's known as a "hi-lo" novel—high interest, low reading level—and in my previous incarnation as a teacher, I might have dismissed it as "too easy" for most of my kids. But I'd broadened my view of what counts as worthwhile reading quite a bit since then. If students liked a book—with a few obvious caveats—it was worth having on the shelves. And every kid who read *Barrio Kings* loved it. Even Bryan—though he didn't broadcast it to anyone.

* * *

By the end of the first semester, a few students had read as many as 15 or 20 books, and most had read at least the 6 that had been required up to that point. More important than the numbers, though, was the increased level of excitement most of them were showing toward reading. They loved watching promotional trailers for new book releases on Fridays. They looked forward to asking questions during the occasional Skype sessions I arranged with young adult authors like Meg Medina and Allison van Diepen. And notes asking me to purchase specific titles started appearing on my desk with increasing frequency: "Can you PLEASE get another copy of SNITCH? Vicky has had it TWO WEEKS and I CANT WAIT! Thank You."

But reading their choice of books wasn't all the students did. I also mixed in targeted lessons on learning root words and new vocabulary, pinpointing an author's purpose, identifying narrative point of view, formulating strong written arguments, and lots more. Some of this involved traditional minilectures and slide shows—not the most thrilling teaching strategies, but I had a lot to squeeze into five 55-minute periods a week. The closer we got to the end of the year and the high-stakes NWEA tests, the more squeezing I found myself doing.

One might think that a veteran teacher with any confidence would be able to ignore the tests. But I couldn't—at least not completely. I didn't want to be the ex-professor whose scores single-handedly caused our school's rating to plummet. I also didn't want to let my students down. As much as I dissed test scores as a true measure of their abilities or intelligence, I knew the kids had been conditioned to see them as important markers of progress. More than that, though, I cared about the scores because I wanted to prove to myself that what I'd preached for years had been right: that you didn't have to teach to the test in order for kids to do well on it.

As winter turned to spring, we were in a steady groove, but I continued to run up against reading resistance in various forms. The most common was students who'd say they completed a book without really doing so. If I got the sense that was the case, I'd ask, "What happened at the end?" Kids who hadn't really finished their book would inevitably act as if they were trying to retrieve the information from a long-closed portal of their brain, then say something like, "Oh, I can't remember the ending," or, even more improbable, "Oh, it's 'cause I read everything except the last chapter." I'd shoot a confounded look, let the student know the jig was up, and give him a few suggestions for a title he might try next.

But they weren't the only ones perpetrating a fraud. One of the ironies of me being a reading teacher was that, in some ways, I didn't practice what I preached. I love to read and do so daily: news, essays, long-form journalism, movie and music reviews, nonfiction, Twitter, commentaries and op-eds, education articles, and comics. But I don't think I've ever read 12 novels cover to cover in the course of a school year—much less 40—even though I require my students to do so. The main reason is that I'm an embarrassingly slow reader—always have been. My wife can read 10 pages in the time it takes me to read 3. But it's also hard to find the time.

Of course, some of my students could, and did, make the same argument, albeit with a different list of responsibilities cramming their daily calendar. When this happened, I tried to be understanding. I knew many were charged with taking care of younger siblings while parents worked second- or third-shift jobs. Some were on soccer teams or folkloric dance squads that practiced after school. I got it. But I held firm to the 20 minutes per day expectation. During the initial round of parent conferences in the fall, I spoke with moms and dads and guardians about it being the centerpiece of our class and asked for their support in checking on their child's progress.

A few days each week, we also devoted 15 minutes of class time to independent reading. At first, it was a struggle, but as students found their passions as readers, it was something they looked forward to and even requested. One day as we were approaching the end of the period, still involved in a discussion about an essay we'd read, Jenny looked up at the clock. "Didn't you say we were gonna read today?" She was waving a copy of Marie Lu's *Legend* in front of her.

"Yeah, you did!' another student chimed in. "We didn't read yesterday, either."

Of course, we'd been reading the entire period, but they meant a different kind: novels of their own choosing. So, a couple minutes later, I sounded a hand chime and the students–save for a couple procrastinators–buried their heads in books of various genres. I did the same. Except for the occasional sniffle or the sound of a turning page, we were enveloped in a beautiful silence.

A couple minutes later, a voice suddenly cut in: "I love this book!" Bryan said out of nowhere and to no one in particular, looking up from his copy of *Eleanor & Park*. "It's heartwarming!"

Yes, Bryan. The kid who'd come in loudly proclaiming his dislike of reading several months earlier, who was one of the "cool kids," who treasured nothing more than his Kevin Durant–model Nikes, was now proclaiming to the entire class not only his love for a book (a romance, at that) but that he found it *heartwarming*. If you don't realize how remarkable that is, you probably haven't taught middle school.

But of course, to the people who counted–the people who liked to count things–Bryan's words didn't matter. I was gratified that most of my students would be leaving my class with a greater love of literature and with more confidence as readers, but those changes couldn't be easily measured. They wouldn't be part of the formula used to determine our school's all-important rating. The only thing that mattered was whether I got the kids' test scores up. If I didn't, I'd be judged a failure by the system, and so would my students. Nothing heartwarming about that.

* * *

Nearly 50 people, mostly parents and siblings of students in my reading class, were packed into our classroom late that spring for an after-school spoken word event. To culminate our poetry unit—and after watching the documentary *Louder Than a Bomb*—students had composed individual and group pieces, then spent 2 weeks revising and rehearsing them. Now they were ready to share them publicly. It was our final big project of the year.

Joel was one of the last to perform. Like Bryan, he had come into the class resistant, and he'd never fully bought into the daily reading routine. But something about the poetry unit had drawn him in, and when it came time to write for the spoken word event, he'd composed not one but two searingly personal pieces about his family. The first was about his fraught relationship with his father and his path toward forgiveness. The second centered on his fierce love for his younger sister, who had epilepsy.

He began, his voice quivering: "My sister's name is Yaritza." And with that simple opening line, tears began rolling down his mother's face. Yaritza cuddled next to her as Joel continued.

> Yari, I don't know if you remember
> But I remember the time you had your first seizure
> I woke up, I saw you shaking, and ran toward you
> I started asking, "Are you OK? Are you OK?"
> Tears running down my face
> "Yari—talk to me, talk to me"
> You opened your eyes and started crying
> I just hugged you tight and said
> Everything's gonna be alright

By the time Joel reached the line "I know I haven't been the best brother to you," his eyes were red, his bottom lip was trembling, and tears were flowing all around the room. His mom and sister, his classmates, other parents, me—we were one big bawling mess. When Joel finished, he brought his hands to his face and covered his eyes. Yari ran up and wrapped her arms around him as the room erupted in applause.

A few days later, Joel and the rest of my reading class filed into the computer lab to take the dreaded NWEA test. Bryan and several other students had worried aloud that they wouldn't make the cut score they needed in order to graduate and move on to high school. As I watched them pore over one lengthy passage after another, hovering their mouse pointers beside empty answer bubbles, I hoped I hadn't let them down.

In the end, their scores were fine. But if you're waiting for me to be more specific than that, to divulge how many met their "growth goal" or what percentage scored above the national average, that's not going to happen. Doing so would only give legitimacy to the idea that test scores really are the best measure of a teacher's (or student's) success, and that is a notion I flatly reject. Suffice it to say I remain convinced that teens become better readers by discovering the joys of reading, and that is most likely to happen when they are given considerable freedom to choose what they read and access to books they find enjoyable and meaningful.

That's not to say that I, or any other teacher in these times, can simply disregard the tests our students are compelled to take. When a single test score can sometimes be what stands between an 8th grader and their high school of choice, it matters quite a lot. A thank-you card Bryan gave me a few days before the end of that year acknowledged as much. "Thanks for helping me do so good on my reading on the NWEA test," he wrote. "Even though you hate it."

A month or so into the next school year, Bryan returned to Quincy to visit. His flowing locks were replaced by a buzz cut, but his smile and easy laugh remained the same. He'd stopped by to check in and let us know he was trying out for the freshman basketball team. He also wanted to know if he could check out a copy of *Eleanor and Park* from my classroom library. He'd told a friend at his high school about it, and she was eager to read it.

CHAPTER SIX

On the Importance of Mirrors—and Windows

The photo was striking. A group of six young children—one boy half-waving and half-hiding, another missing a tooth, several holding up two-fingered peace signs, all mugging for the camera. Their sandals were scuffed and muddy, the ground beneath them just brown dirt and tiny gravel. Behind them, blurred by the shot's shallow focus, tent ropes jutted diagonally into the frame on both sides.

A class of 7th graders studied the photo and typed notes in two columns: "windows" on the left and "mirrors" on the right. After a couple minutes, I broke the silence: "Who can share a mirror that you found?"

"They're all together smiling for the picture, and I've taken pictures like that with my cousins," said Alex.

"They look like they're wearing *chanclas*," Emma said. Several students giggled at her use of the word, heard commonly in Mexican households but not so often in school. "And I have *chanclas*, too."

"Okay, good—how about windows?" I asked. "Who saw something in the photo that wasn't familiar to you?"

"Their shoes and pants are really dirty," Diana said. "Like maybe they haven't washed them in a long time. And I don't see any grass—just dirt."

"And in the back it looks like there's a bunch of tents," Sergio added. "Maybe they're living there and I've never lived in a tent."

I asked where they thought the photo might've been taken. We discussed the meaning of the word *refugee* and why the kids in the picture might be smiling even though they seemed to be living in difficult conditions. Then we examined several more photographs, one at a time, seeking out windows and mirrors in each: uniformed students doing math problems in a Nigerian school; a Latinx family and friends gathered for a summer picnic on a city sidewalk; a gay couple moments before their wedding; Pakistani women praying at a mosque; and police officers surrounded by evidence markers on a Chicago street corner. For each picture, the same questions: What's familiar? What's not? How can you connect to the people in the photo?

I first saw the terms *window* and *mirror* used in this sense in a book chapter by Peggy McIntosh and Emily Style.[1] But the idea had been birthed even earlier, in 1990, by Rudine Sims Bishop.[2] She wrote of the dearth of children's books featuring people of color, and of the potential for multicultural literature to serve as a mirror of "self-affirmation" for Black and brown kids. It became one of my favorite metaphors, and I'd used it with middle schoolers, undergrads, and to reflect on my own teaching. Schools should be places where kids explore the unfamiliar but also see their own lived experiences validated and valued. For students whose racial, cultural, linguistic, or economic backgrounds differ significantly from that of mainstream White America, the "mirrors" can be particularly powerful.

But mirrors for students of color are frequently in short supply. Take this simple example: A Google search for "hand" brings up row after row of images of white-skinned hands. You'll even scroll past a silicon hand, a mummified hand, and a "hand that started rotting after eating sushi" before you get to a brown or black person's hand. Search for "nose" or "mouth" and the results are largely the same. This sort of underrepresentation—whether found in online resources, the books on classroom shelves, curriculum requirements, or the teachers students see every day—is widespread in schools. But too many White educators don't see it as a problem.

In an online essay titled "My School District Hires Too Many White Teachers,"[3] Glenn Sullivan, a Black 19-year-old from New Orleans, observes that the percentage of Black teachers in New Orleans's schools plummeted due to post-Hurricane Katrina reform efforts, with a corresponding rise in "teachers from outside the city," many of whom were

White. Sullivan argues that in a school system where nearly 90% of students are African American, Black teachers are vital because they are often better able to connect with their students. He cites one of his teachers, Mr. Allen, who "used language and cultural references that we recognized to challenge and inspire us." What young people need, Sullivan concludes, is teachers who "truly understand the environment that students come from—rather than just knowing the statistics that describe their lives."[4]

One reason Sullivan's piece resonated with me was that a similar transformation in teacher demographics had happened in Chicago schools since my first go-round as a teacher. In 2000, 40% of the city's public school teachers were Black. By 2015—after nearly 2 decades of corporate-style reform efforts that featured an influx of young, White teachers—only 23% were Black.[5] School closings, which disproportionately targeted Black neighborhoods on Chicago's south side, had led to even more Black teachers losing their jobs.

So, I thought Sullivan's argument was on point. What he was talking about was the importance of mirrors in the ranks of teachers—that kids need to see their own lives and cultural experiences reflected in those who engage them in learning. But some teachers saw it differently. After the piece was posted on the Facebook page of a national teacher advocacy group, it generated hundreds of comments. Many were critical of Sullivan's essay.

"Garbage. I don't give a shit what color your skin is as long as you can teach," one commenter wrote.

"Instead of being appreciative that there are people out there willing to give their all and teach kids, the child is focused on color. Not ok!" wrote another.

"In a word, BS," another commenter added. "Color doesn't matter. A good teacher is a good teacher regardless of race, sex, or anything else."

I didn't know for certain that these sentiments, and many others like them, were all posted by White teachers. But it wasn't going out on a limb to guess that they were. I'd heard White teachers say similar things over the years, and I thought it a was safe bet to assume that many (and possibly all) of those reacting negatively to Sullivan's essay were White.

I could understand, on some level, why that might happen. They take it personally. They feel attacked or misunderstood. But for White teachers to disregard the perspective of a Black student so swiftly and even callously is concerning. It reveals a lack of awareness about—or an unwillingness to seriously confront—issues of race and how they impact the experiences of students of color. And it also points to an aversion to critical self-reflection—an important asset for all educators that may be even more vital for White teachers.

I'd seen firsthand the importance of students having teachers who they can connect with on a cultural level. Although I do my best to build strong bonds with my Latinx students, I'm not able to do so in the way some of my Mexican American colleagues can. When Cudberto Esparza, Quincy's upper grade math teacher, calls a student "m'ijo" or banters with kids in the hallway about which Mexican soccer team is best ("Chivas!" "No, América!"), there's a shared cultural kinship that says, in effect, "I know where you're coming from." Nancy Ibarra elicits similar feelings from students when she reads stories she's written about her own life during Writers' Workshop. The same was true when I taught in a mostly Black school. My colleague Roy Ousley knew what it meant to grow up Black and male in Chicago in ways I never could—and our male students recognized and appreciated it. That kind of deep, experiential understanding matters in the classroom. When students feel culturally connected, they tend to feel safe and respected. When they feel safe and respected, they're better able to learn.

That doesn't mean it's impossible for me to be a good teacher to my students or that someone who shares their racial or cultural background would be better by default. But to say that a teacher's race is of no importance is saying that mirrors don't matter for young people. Yet they do.

* * *

Many teachers are familiar with the work of Walter Dean Myers, a celebrated author of over 100 books for teens and children who died in 2014. Most of Myers's young adult novels are set in Harlem and feature Black (and sometimes Latinx) teens struggling against the kinds of challenges that often confront my 7th and 8th graders. Students in my classes—especially boys—love Myers's novels and can relate to his characters. Books like *Monster, Slam!*, and *Lockdown* typically engage even the most reluctant readers.

A couple days after Myers's death, I stumbled upon Alexander Nazaryan's 2012 blog post, "Against Walter Dean Myers and the dumbing down of literature."[6] Nazaryan, who was then a senior writer at *Newsweek*, taught middle school and high school in Brooklyn for several years prior to his career as a journalist. In his post, he remembers his students devouring Myers's work as eagerly as mine do. But Nazaryan saw this as troubling. Myers's books, he says, are "painfully mundane, with simple moral lessons built into predictable situations: the projects, prison, redemption." They fail to make kids think deeply, he writes, because "they are about those kids' own sad lives."[7]

In Nazaryan's educational universe, mirrors aren't only unnecessary for children in city schools—they're an obstacle, a crutch. But while he sees only the characters' "sad lives" in Myers's books, Myers himself viewed his work through a much different lens. In a 1986 piece for the *New York Times*, he wrote that being a Black writer of books for young people meant

> understanding the nuances of value, of religion, of dreams. It meant capturing the subtle rhythms of language and movement and weaving it all, the sound and the gesture, the sweat and the prayers, into the recognizable fabric of black life.[8]

Nazaryan proposes that instead of teaching Myers, urban teachers should do what he did at the Brooklyn Latin School: teach Homer and Virgil. The classics. I've never read more than a line or two of Virgil, so Nazaryan would no doubt discount my thoughts on the matter, but I found his post to be both elitist and wrongheaded. I was dismayed to see him so casually dismiss the work of a Black author whose books have been a lifeline—and an entryway to a love of literature—for countless Black and Latinx teens. But beyond that, I disagreed with his central thesis: that young people in city schools can be intellectually challenged only by the so-called classics.

The 7th and 8th graders I teach are provoked, challenged, and (to use Nazaryan's term) "elevated" by a wide range of contemporary literature and nonfiction—from Angie Thomas's *The Hate U Give* and Benjamin Alire Saenz's *Aristotle and Dante Discover the Secrets of the Universe* to the poetry of Danez Smith and Mayda Del Valle. Occasionally, we read something from the "classic" canon, too, but many of those texts spend more time gathering dust in the book closet.

But this isn't just about Nazaryan or a handful of teachers in an online forum. If we look at the bigger picture, it's clear that the lack of concern about inclusion and representation infects schools at a systemic level as well. The belief that "a good teacher is a good teacher—race doesn't matter" morphs into realities like this one: In Chicago charter schools in 2011, 95% of students were black or Latinx, while 70% of their teachers were White.[9] Similar imbalances are common in children's and young adult literature titles. The Cooperative Children's Book Center reviewed 3,700 books published for children and teens in 2017. Of those, only 250 were written by Black or Latinx authors.[10]

The point here is not that Black and Latinx students shouldn't have White teachers or read literature by authors of European heritage. After all, the metaphor points toward mirrors *and* windows. But the presence of racial and cultural mirrors for students of color needs to be seen as a necessity, not a luxury or an afterthought. For school administrators, that means being intentional and persistent about hiring more Black and brown teachers and counselors. For department or grade-level chairs, it means increased availability of ethnic studies courses, wide representation of authors of color in English classes, and making explicit cultural and global connections in syllabi for math, sciences, and the arts. For teachers, it means looking closely at unit plans, bookshelves, assignments, and special programs to ensure that students of color feel validated and see themselves and their cultural backgrounds represented in authentic ways. And for all White educators, it means making efforts to rectify our own lack of knowledge and understanding when it comes to matters of race.

* * *

The population of the United States may be becoming more diverse by the year, but a large number of White teachers spent their formative years in racial and cultural houses of mirrors. Most went to K–12 schools in White neighborhoods or towns, where White teachers taught White history and White literature, while White cultural norms guided nearly every aspect of educational and social life. None of this was by choice. They were kids; it was their experience by default. But as adults, many of us have more control over our life's trajectory, and when we realize we have been miseducated, it's on us to do something about it. That means White educators need to seek out as many windows as they can find.

Too often, though, White teachers appear less than eager to do so. On Twitter, Black and brown teachers use the platform to keep issues of educational equity and inclusion in the mix. Educolor, for example, an online collective cofounded by New York City teacher and author Jose Vilson, hosts monthly chats where teachers from across the country (some of them White) discuss topics that aren't getting much play elsewhere on EduTwitter, such as "Immigration, Deportations, and Education" and "Engaging and Supporting Parents of Color."[11] But many White teachers, I've noticed, steer clear of such chats. They're much more likely to engage with tweets on instructional or organizational topics (like how to design an "awesome" anchor chart) than those about social or educational inequities that impact Black and brown children (like the school-to-prison pipeline). Tweet a photo of hand-painted supply bins in various colors, and you'll get dozens of likes from White teachers. Tweet about the need for more teachers of color, and you'll likely get crickets from the same folks.

Yes, I'm overgeneralizing. White allies and advocates and accomplices are out there. I try, both inside and outside my classroom, to be one. But far too many White educators are silent on issues of racial equity and justice—not just on social media but in their school buildings and their out-of-school lives. Based on what I learned from working with hundreds of White prospective teachers when I was a professor, this aversion to confronting race likely stems in part from feelings of inadequacy due to ignorance. Many White people are aware, though they may not admit it, that their own knowledge of other cultures and histories is shallow at best, and in some cases virtually nonexistent.

Fear is also a factor for White teachers—fear that engaging in conversations about the intersections of race, culture, and educational equity will end up with accusatory fingers pointed at them. They're the problem; they're the racists. But the fear of being labeled a racist masks a more uncomfortable truth: Every White person, consciously or not, benefits from racism. Every White person who grows up in the United States internalizes racist stereotypes about people of color from an early age. (This happens to people of color, too, in different ways, but here I'm speaking primarily about White teachers.) We all carry around racist baggage of varying weights. Pretending otherwise doesn't make it any less real.

In her now-classic book, *Why Are All the Black Kids Sitting Together in the Cafeteria?,*[12] Beverly Daniel Tatum compares the continuing cycle of racism in the United States to an airport's moving walkway. Even if people stand still on the walkway, Tatum says, they are still being pulled in the direction of a society marked by racist structures, beliefs, and actions. The only way to break free from it, even partially, is to walk in the other direction—to be purposefully antiracist.

So, how does a White teacher do that? School districts typically give minimal attention to developing the capacities of White teachers to draw upon the cultural experiences of students of color, or to view their work in the classroom through an antiracist lens. While occasional workshops related to cultural proficiency or antibias teaching may be offered, little emphasis is placed on their importance systemwide. In school buildings where the quest to keep test scores up is paramount, administrators often focus professional development sessions on narrow, instruction-centered topics.

But that shouldn't let White teachers off the hook. If your school doesn't provide you with adequate materials to teach science, good teachers don't say, "Well, I just won't teach science." They seek out resources on their own. They search online. They read articles and books. They consult with colleagues who have more expertise in the area. The same should hold true for White teachers when it comes to cultural competency and racial equity: Seek out resources. Read books exclusively by authors of color for a year. Follow educators of color on Twitter and listen to what they have to say. Gather other White colleagues for a book group on Robin DiAngelo's *White Fragility.* Check out websites of organizations like *Teaching Tolerance* and *Rethinking Schools.* Make it a point not to spend so much time in all-White spaces. Examine your curriculum for explicit or implicit bias. Speak out against inequitable practices and policies in your school. Share what you're doing with other teachers. And repeat.

The larger point is that deepening one's understanding of issues of race and culture isn't something that happens in a single PD session or a weekend viewing of *The Blind Side.* It's an ongoing commitment. I've spent nearly 30 years working in and with Chicago schools, almost exclusively with Latinx and Black students, and I'm still doing the work, still have a lot to learn. For the most part, though, it is undertaken on my own or in conversation with thoughtful colleagues—not as part of efforts my school district has initiated.

* * *

The crux of the matter is this: 82% of public school teachers and 80% of administrators in U.S. schools are White.[13] When so many White educators live their lives in houses of mirrors, we end up with classrooms, schools, and districts that are not attending to issues of equity and racial justice in meaningful and sustained ways. Yes, many educators of color do their best to carry the load, but it shouldn't be on them to shoulder all the work. In fact, since White people, historically, have been responsible for creating the inequitable conditions in our schools, we have an even greater responsibility to make things right. That means going far beyond surface-level efforts at "celebrating diversity." It means ensuring that schools are committed to being fully inclusive, anti-racist spaces.

We have a long way to go before we get there. But good things are happening. Although publishers of books and curriculum for young people continue to play catch up in providing authentic mirrors for Black and brown kids, educators of color aren't waiting around for them. Debbie Reese has long provided critical analysis of children's books about indigenous people on her website, American Indians in Children's Literature.[14] More recent grassroots efforts—also led, not coincidentally, by women of color—are building upon Reese's work. #WeNeedDiverseBooks[15] amplifies the need for wider representation in children's and young adult literature by highlighting newly published titles, supporting authors from marginalized communities with grants and mentoring, and bringing books and authors into schools. #DisruptTexts[16] challenges teachers to question stereotypical characterizations, problematic plot lines, and cultural erasure in so-called classic literature, and to replace or pair such texts with counter-narratives. Valeria Brown's #ClearTheAir[17] features regular Twitter chats—often focused on issues of race, equity, power, and privilege in education—that encourage participants from various backgrounds to engage in honest discourse and hold one another accountable. In addition, several state governments have, in the past few years, passed legislation requiring some form of ethnic studies in schools—from required electives for high school students to comprehensive K–12 curriculums.

In her widely viewed TED talk, "The Danger of a Single Story,"[18] novelist and essayist Chimamanda Ngozi Adichie remembers that the stories she wrote as a child in Nigeria were filled with blue-eyed White children who ate apples and played in the snow. Why? Because those were the people and situations she had read about in the British and American children's books that were available to her back then: all windows—no mirrors. She thought books had to be about people unlike those she knew in her own life. But as she grew older, reading the works of African authors opened her eyes. "Because of writers like Chinua Achebe and Camara Laye, I went through a mental shift in my perception of literature," she says. "I realized that people like me, girls with skin the color of chocolate, whose kinky hair could not form ponytails, could also exist in literature. I started to write about things I recognized."[19] And the world is better for it. Adichie has crafted much-needed literary mirrors for Nigerian and other African women in her novels, as well as indelible windows for millions of other readers.

White teachers might not be able to create mirrors for students of color like Adichie and other authors—and teachers—of color can. But surely we can understand their importance. We can take them seriously. We can seek them out. And we can make it an essential part of our work to hold them up.

CHAPTER SEVEN

Test and Punish

Probation.

In the trampled landscape of American public schools, it is a dreaded label, a badge of dishonor, a scarlet letter. It's a warning shot fired by a district or state accreditation agency toward a school and its staff, and the message is simple: Get your students' test scores up, or else.

In Chicago, the "or else" meant being "turned around"—taken over by a completely new administration and set of teachers—or being shut down altogether. Both had been standard features of the city's reform playbook, and for a few years, each spring had brought another round of contested school closures—almost always in low-income Black or Latinx communities. In most cases, the first step in the process was probation, which seemed less like a carrot or stick than a sledgehammer. It wasn't always a death sentence, but it felt like it.

At least that was what I'd heard. And when our principal called us all into the gym for a meeting one afternoon to inform us that the warning shot had been fired at us, that we—Quincy—been put on probation, that's pretty much how it was. Anxiety levels ratcheted up a few notches, accompanied by a somber sense of dread. It didn't sound good, and it didn't feel good. Of course, it wasn't supposed to.

The saddest thing about it, to me, was how quickly the "probation" label shifted the way some of the adults at our school viewed our collective work. If, the day before, you'd asked individual teachers whether they thought our school was a "good" one, most would have said yes without hesitation. After the probationary designation, though, some seemed to accept the notion that we'd somehow been wrong about ourselves all along, that the board's formula for measuring school failure was infallible, that we were indeed on a wayward ship that needed immediate course correction.

Even if you didn't buy into that line of thinking—and I didn't—it was hard not to feel added pressure. If we weren't able to climb out of the probationary cellar after the first year, we'd be much more likely to be turned around, which would mean a complete reboot, with all teachers and administrators losing their jobs. I was a little worried about how that could affect me personally, but I was more concerned about what it would mean for the community. Quincy was nearly 120 years old. Generations of immigrant families had sent their children through its doors. It was a valued and valuable asset in the neighborhood, a site of hope and a safe haven. I didn't want to see it be overtaken by a gung-ho charter operator or a battalion of Teach for America recruits.

Besides, being turned around wasn't the only threat. Like many other schools in the city, we were already facing enrollment declines thanks to the glut of new charter schools, some of which were brazen in their recruitment efforts. The week before the academic year began, representatives from a nearby, soon-to-open charter had passed out promotional brochures to parents right across the street from our school.

Budget cuts and layoffs were also impacting schools across the city. Many no longer had librarians. Others, like ours, had a social worker who had to split time among two or three buildings, so students with urgent needs—like self-harm or sexual abuse—often had to wait a week for a session. Teachers tried to fill the void, of course, and the Chicago Teachers Union leadership fought to stem the losses, but the bottom line was that teachers were being asked to do more with less. At one CTU rally against proposed budget reductions that I attended, a teacher held a sign that read:

> Dear students,
>
> Due to recent budget cuts, please bring the following supplies on the 1st day of classes:
>
> toilet paper
> paper towels

markers
1 case copy paper
hand soap
books
pencils
teachers
teachers' aides
nurse

The irony was impossible to miss: On one hand, CPS schools like ours were being warned that we needed to improve test scores or face dire consequences; on the other, funding that could provide vital resources for students was being cut. All of these larger contexts swirled around our hallways and through our classrooms each day. I tried to set them aside and focus on the kids in front of me, but it was sometimes difficult to do so completely.

* * *

Because CPS used both the NWEA/MAP test and the ISAT (Illinois Standards Achievement Test) to make high-stakes decisions about student promotion and "school quality," they caused particular worry for students and teachers. So, when the district announced that the spring 2014 administration of the ISAT would be its last—and would have no high stakes attached to it—teachers welcomed the news. The relief was fleeting, though. The ISAT was being bumped in favor of a soon-to-come, Common Core–aligned, "next generation" assessment known as PARCC. Anyone who thought things couldn't get any worse when it came to testing in public schools would soon be proven wrong.

With no stakes attached to the lame duck ISAT, a coalition of parent and community groups called More Than a Score began urging parents to sign letters opting their children out of the test. Around the city, hundreds of parents did so. Many seemed to view the opt-out movement not only as a statement against the ISAT but as a revolt against the entire top-down, market-based, test-driven direction CPS schools had taken over the preceding decade.

Similar grassroots resistance to standardized testing was bubbling up across the country. In part, it was a reaction to over-testing—the sheer number of hours kids were forced to spend taking numerous multi-day assessments and the resulting loss of learning time. But an even stronger argument against the tests, at least for me, was that they serve as a sorting mechanism that privileges White and wealthier students while disadvantaging low-income kids and students of color. As Jesse Hagopian, who, along with other Seattle teachers and students, led a successful boycott of the NWEA's MAP test, writes, "what standardized tests measure above all else is a student's access to resources. The most damning truth about standardized tests is that they are a better indicator of a student's zip code than a student's aptitude."[1]

At Quincy, a few of us discussed ways to ensure that more parents in our school's community were aware of the opt-out option, but the idea didn't gain much traction for two reasons: Some teachers were ambivalent about giving the ISAT a final time and just wanted to get it over with; others were understandably fearful of losing their jobs if they challenged the test. I worried about that, too, but I also wanted to be sure parents in the neighborhood were informed of their options. So, after school one day, Kim Goldbaum and I distributed informational flyers about the opt-out movement to parents picking up their children—across the street, off school property. I also gave some to Sister Angie Kolacinski, a long-time community activist, who made them available for parents who were interested. In the days that followed, over three dozen Quincy students submitted opt-out forms.

As momentum continued to build just a week before the ISAT was scheduled to begin, a group of teachers from Saucedo Scholastic Academy, also on the south side, raised the stakes even higher. They held a press conference announcing that they planned to boycott the ISAT.[2] News reports said as many as two dozen teachers at the school had agreed not to give the test, and hundreds of Saucedo students intended to opt out as well. CPS's chief executive officer, Barbara Byrd-Bennett, responded by threatening disciplinary action—including possible revocation of state teaching licenses—but the Saucedo teachers didn't budge. A few days later, teachers at another CPS school, Drummond, said they would join the boycott.[3]

Watching all this unfold, I felt like a phony. For years I'd spoken out against the abuses of high-stakes tests. I'd written op-eds. I'd talked about it in presentations and appeared on panels. I'd encouraged prospective teachers I'd taught to find ways to resist the pressure of teaching to the test once they had classrooms of their own. But here I was, standing on the sidelines as other teachers put their jobs on the line. It didn't feel right.

I knew, as the Saucedo and Drummond organizers obviously did, that there was strength in numbers. But I doubted we could convince even a small group of teachers at my school to join the boycott, especially since we were on probation. Folks were already concerned about losing their jobs—they didn't need another reason. Tension in the building was high. I thought briefly about boycotting by myself, but that seemed too risky. It hadn't been long since I'd given up a tenure-track university position to return to CPS as a nontenured teacher. I didn't want to be without work. So, with gritted teeth, I walked into my classroom the following Monday morning with a box of ISAT test booklets under my arm.

That's when I learned that, over the weekend, our school's list of nearly 40 students whose parents had signed opt-out letters had somehow been whittled down to fewer than 10. What? How had that happened? Maybe a few older kids had signed the letters themselves without informing their parents, but I couldn't imagine more than a handful had done that. What about all the others? Why the last-minute change of heart? Something was foul.

And we soon discovered that it wasn't only at our school. Kim heard via a text from a friend that parents at a number of schools on the south and west sides had received phone calls "strongly encouraging" them not to opt their children out. Some students said their parents were told the school would lose funding if their child didn't take the test. Others said they were told that the school could forfeit teaching positions. I didn't know exactly where the directive had come from, but if it was happening at schools in different areas, it seemed clear that someone at the district level was calling the shots.

I was fuming inside—not only because the opt-out numbers had been diminished but because tactics like those wouldn't be attempted with middle-class or wealthy parents. It was patronizing and indefensible. But like CPS's repeated threats against boycotting teachers, this response had little to do with the ISAT itself. The test was as good as buried. What district leaders were trying desperately to protect was the edifice of corporate-style school reform. Testing was the base that the entire house of cards rested on, and if boycotts and opt-outs were allowed to succeed on a wide scale, the whole deck could come tumbling down.

But I didn't have the luxury of focusing on that for long. Moments after getting the news from Kim, a woman walked into my room and informed me she'd been sent to proctor my test session. *What the . . . ?* Upper grade classrooms almost never had proctors at Quincy, so the reason for her presence seemed clear: I was being monitored. I walked down the hall to confirm my suspicions, and sure enough: Kim and another teacher on my team who'd been vocal about the opt-out movement had been assigned proctors as well. Soon thereafter, I got a two-word text from Kim. "I'm out," it said. She had left the building in protest. The proctor was the final straw.

It should have been for me, too. But as the appointed time for the test approached, I stood by the intercom button, unsure of what to do. Should I walk out, too? Should I buzz the office and tell them, as my students watched and listened, that I was refusing to give the test? Or should I cool off and take the night to think things over? I knew my 7th graders could tell something was wrong, that I was agitated, angry. I felt bad that I might be making them nervous or uneasy when the assessment was about to begin, but the truth was, it didn't matter how they performed. The test didn't count. All this craziness over a doomed assessment.

The seconds ticked away as testing time got closer. My finger hovered over the intercom button. At the last moment, I pulled it back.

"Break the seal on your test booklets and turn to page 2," I said, checking the clock. I read the rest of the directions aloud, but my head was somewhere else entirely. My students—except for the single kid in my homeroom who was still opting out—began the ISAT. I felt like a coward.

* * *

The next morning, after talking it over with my wife, Lisa, I came in and told my principal that I couldn't, in good conscience, give the test for the rest of the week. I was boycotting. I also informed my homeroom students, saying I hoped they understood that I was standing up for what I thought was right—for them and for me—and that I wouldn't do anything I believed would have negative repercussions for them or the school.

"What's gonna happen to you?" one asked.

"I don't know," I said. "I guess we'll see."

Instead of being sent home or banished to a dungeon for delinquent teachers, I was charged with supervising the opt-out kids while the rest of the students took the test each day. Essentially, this meant sitting with them in the school's barren lunchroom for a couple hours while they read or wrote or sketched or otherwise kept themselves busy. I'd heard about teachers at other schools turning their opt-out rooms into fun, makeshift learning labs, but I didn't have the mental or emotional energy left to make that happen.

Before the reading/writing/art time began each day, I had one required duty: Read aloud the long-winded introductory language to the ISAT to the assembled opt-out students. "You will have 50 minutes . . . wah, wah, wah . . . read the directions carefully . . . wah, wah, wah . . . continue working . . . wah, wah, wah . . . when you have finished . . . wah, wah, wah." Even to my own ears, I sounded like Charlie Brown's teacher. After going through the entire routine, I'd say, "You may begin." They would then respond in unison, "I refuse to take the test." At that point I would collect the test booklets, and the curtain would close on the production.

Why this charade was required I'm still not exactly sure (something to do with releasing CPS from liability, no doubt), but I had to do it three times each morning—once for each grade level of out-opt kids. I always ended with the 5th grader—there was only one—and when I'd get to the "You may begin" part, he would start giggling uncontrollably instead of saying his line. It usually took me a couple minutes to get him to actually say aloud, "I refuse to take the test."

One night that week, I sent a lengthy email to all the teachers at my school, explaining why I'd decided to boycott and emphasizing that it wasn't a decision I had made lightly or recklessly. Only a few colleagues responded. In the halls, I felt a chilly reception from coworkers who normally would at least say hello. Even one of my close friends expressed disappointment. "I really wish you hadn't done that," he told me.

I was caught between two feelings I didn't like: Part of me felt like I hadn't done enough, that I should have walked out on Day One and encouraged others to do the same; another part regretted that many of my colleagues seemed to feel let down or even betrayed by my actions. They were concerned, I figured, that my protest would somehow end up hurting our chances of getting off probation. But the lack of support was emblematic of the palpable sense of fear that permeates so many school buildings in the age of test-and-punish reform. "Everybody's afraid," a CPS teacher friend once told me. "Until we get over that fear, it's going to be hard to make a change."

For much of the rest of that school year, I felt like something of an outcast. I'm sure some of it was my own heightened sensitivity, but it was there nonetheless. The cloud of probation was still hovering overhead, of course, so that didn't help matters any. The generalized sense of dread in the building was still high. We were all on edge about what would happen if that year's test scores didn't go up.

It wasn't until the next school year, when Quincy was officially removed from probation by CPS, that a collective exhale was heard. The skies cleared. We all relaxed a bit. I was still a little worried that the hammer of punishment was going to drop on Kim and me because of our boycott, but it never came. Ironically, a different hammer did eventually fall—on Barbara Byrd-Bennett, the chief executive officer of CPS at the time, who had issued the earlier threats to boycotting teachers. Later that year, facing a 23-count indictment for orchestrating a multi-million-dollar kickback scheme while at CPS, Byrd-Bennett pleaded guilty. She was sentenced to four and a half years in federal prison.[4]

CHAPTER EIGHT

When the World Hands Us Curriculum

While planning for the coming year late one August night, I began to see tweets about unrest in a town I'd never heard of: Ferguson, Missouri. At the time, the details were just trickling out. A Black teenager had been killed by a police officer. Residents were angry. According to early reports, the teen had been unarmed, and his body had been left in the street for hours.

I stayed up late that night, and the next, and several more over the following week watching live feeds and checking updates on Twitter. I was transfixed by what was happening and what it might mean for our country: another police killing of an unarmed Black person, an outraged community, growing resistance, police in riot gear, tear gas aimed at protesters, and military vehicles patrolling the streets. It seemed too important to ignore, and I decided to ditch what I had been planning and begin our year in social studies with the killing of Michael Brown.

I had long incorporated current events in my curriculum, no matter what subject I was teaching: media, reading/language arts, or social studies. But in my 1990s incarnation, my conception of doing so was different. I generally focused on broader topics—media bias, racism, gender discrimination, immigration, gun control, environmental concerns. The Ferguson unit would deviate from that approach in that it would be centered on a singular conflict that was still unfolding as we studied it. That gave it more urgency, to be sure, but it also made it more challenging to plan and potentially even more problematic to teach.

Even in the years before the unit on Ferguson, I'd wanted my students to see, right from the beginning of the year, that "social studies" wasn't only about the past—it was about what was happening in the world right then, their community and their lives, justice and injustice in the present moment. We delved into history, of course, but we never became stuck there. We plumbed its conflicts for lessons we could use in today's world. We tried to draw lines of connection from past fights for equality and dignity to current struggles. But while those had been my guideposts all along, Michael Brown's killing made them more pressing priorities. More and more, I began to see my social studies classes as an answer to a question teacher and author Sara Ahmed posed on Twitter: "How do we respond when the world hands us curriculum?"[1]

It can be tempting to respond by turning away, by convincing ourselves that delving into contentious current topics is a minefield we aren't prepared to cross. And that may, in some cases, be a reasonable course. If it turns out that we aren't ready for what gets stirred up in class, our lessons, however well intentioned, may end up doing more harm than good.[2] Especially when exploring issues that have a direct impact on students' lives, emotions can be raw. And in classrooms where kids come from multiple racial, cultural, or economic backgrounds, current events can become the proverbial can of worms. Even in less obviously diverse spaces, like my classroom of mostly Mexican immigrant kids, caution is warranted, building trust is essential, and thinking through possible difficult scenarios ahead of time is a must. Still, challenges may arise.

After all, teaching something for the first time is always hard. When you are truly ripping lessons from the headlines, constructing learning around events that have just happened or are still developing, the way forward is even more uncertain. Early news reports can be inaccurate. Conflicting accounts sometimes emerge. Gathering reliable sources can be difficult (though Black Twitter and crowd-sourced curricula like #FergusonSyllabus[3] have made it a much less solitary endeavor). But despite these possible pitfalls, to avoid teaching about the most important issues of our time is, for me, not an option. When I watched armored trucks roll through Ferguson spraying tear gas on people protesting a police officer's killing of a Black teen, I felt strongly that I couldn't *not* teach about it.

Of course, some would say that in making such curricular decisions, I am imposing these topics and conversations on my students. I would argue that every curricular decision is a choice, informed either consciously or not by a teacher's racial and cultural lenses, life experiences, biases, and beliefs. Some teachers might counter that they have no choice in what to teach—they are compelled to follow the curriculum their district requires. Even so, somebody is making the choices about what's being studied, and it's almost never the kids. Unless students are truly directing their own learning and choosing topics to explore, teaching about the events in Ferguson or Charlottesville is no more an imposition than teaching about the different types of prairies.

Besides, since social studies wasn't a subject that showed up on high-stakes tests, CPS gave it scant attention. When schools met to craft their improvement plans every 2 years, they chose from a menu of district-approved "focus areas" to direct their attention, but unlike other academic subjects, social studies wasn't even on the list. For several years, our school had "vertical teams" of teachers who huddled in biweekly meetings focused on reading, math, science, and writing—but social studies was a ghost. It was freeing, in a sense, because I had more leeway in laying out a plan for my classes. But it was troubling as well. If our schools were supposed to be preparing informed, democratic citizens, how could we relegate social studies to a curricular afterthought?

* * *

Our unit on Michael Brown's killing and the protests that followed ended up spiraling outward and lasting longer than I'd planned. We examined primary sources. We studied the legal standards regarding police use of force. We considered questions about the First Amendment rights of protesters and the media. We explored the history of redlining and segregation in St. Louis and its suburbs. We discussed the conflicting philosophies underlying a rallying cry of protesters—"No justice, no peace"—and the words of Missouri's governor, Jay Nixon: "If we are going to achieve justice, we must first have and maintain peace."[4] We analyzed tweets using the #IfTheyGunnedMeDown hashtag and the lyrics of J. Cole's "Be Free." And we drew parallels between the uprising of citizens in Ferguson and a concurrent wave of protests across Mexico, where 43 college students, all training to be teachers, were massacred and then "disappeared" near the town of Iguala.

When the unit finally ended, I told my students we'd continue to circle back to Michael Brown's killing—and the larger issue of police violence against Black Americans—throughout the year. So, in December, my 8th graders entered the classroom to see a website headline screaming from the whiteboard: *Grand Jury Declines to Indict NYPD Officer in Eric Garner Chokehold Death.*

"What does that mean—that they didn't indict?" Nidia asked.

"They're saying the cop's not guilty," Cristiano said.

"You're close," I said. "They're saying they're not going to charge him with a crime."

A quiet moment or two passed—what I read as a partially stunned silence. Then:

"Bogus!" someone called out.

"They're racist."

"Seems like no matter what the evidence is, they always say the same thing: It wasn't a crime."

"Didn't they watch the video?" Nidia asked. She and a number of other students had seen the footage online: New York City police officers tackling Garner and putting him in a fatal choke hold as he pleaded, time and again, for air. "How can they not indict with that video, that evidence? What are they looking at?"

I sensed that many students were feeling some mixture of sadness and anger, once again let down by a systemic failure to render justice in what, to most of them, seemed a clear-cut case. With a few minutes left in the period, I asked them to write on an index card either questions they still had about the grand jury's decision or a short reflection on what they thought about it. The final question Celi scribbled on her card accomplished both in six words:

Why do we let this happen?

It was a great question, and one that's hard to answer in a way that might satisfy a 13-year-old—or anybody else, really. Why *do* we let it happen? The way she'd turned the dilemma back on all of us, rather than just the perpetrators, was particularly damning. Her question stayed with me over the next couple days—so much so that I posted a photo of her index card on Twitter.

Within minutes, out came the trolls. "Teacher should tell the students to obey the police, not resist them," a user known as "D.B." wrote. "Explain to them that Eric Garner resisted arrest and Michael Brown attacked a policeman before they died . . . Teach them facts not propaganda."

In almost every case, I ignore provocations such as this on Twitter. I don't find it to be a useful forum for debate, and most people don't want to have a genuine discussion anyway. They want to talk, not listen. But for some reason, this time I took the bait.

"[My students] are well aware of what happened in both cases," I responded. "Nearly all still think both were crimes."

D.B. again: "Because their teacher is reinforcing it and is teaching them propaganda and not facts and evidence. . . . They are not aware of what happened, just what their angry teacher told them." He added, "Do you think you're protecting them by teaching them lies?"

I should have just let it go. But I didn't. "No, actually I almost never use the social studies textbook so I think I'm protecting them from lies."

By this point, a couple other Twitter acquaintances had jumped to my defense, arguing that I was pushing my students to think critically. But D.B. wasn't having it: "You should stick to teaching recess on the playground," he wrote. "Stay out of classrooms . . . you are teaching propaganda and not facts. Don't lie to students."

The futile back and forth reminded me why I usually didn't engage in Twitter spats. But the issue D.B. raised—the power of a teacher to indoctrinate rather than educate students, and the potentially thin line between the two—was something I thought about quite a bit. Although his snap judgment emerged out of baseless assumptions, I knew the question underlying it was more complicated than many teachers want to admit. I decided it might be a good idea to bring my students in on the conversation, and I let D.B. know. "I may use this entire [Twitter] conversation as our curriculum for tomorrow," I tweeted. "You will be part of the lesson!"

* * *

The next day, when the class came in, I had the words "education" and "indoctrination" displayed on the whiteboard. I asked if they knew what they meant. Several students provided decent definitions of "education" ("learning things you don't know," "being taught something new," "the process of learning"), but when I asked about "indoctrination," nobody volunteered an answer. Prepared for that possibility, I revealed a definition on the next slide: "Any form of teaching that instills beliefs in students in such a way that they are unwilling or unable to question or evaluate those beliefs independently."

"Oh, I heard of that before," David said. "Like brainwashing."

"What do you mean by that?"

Yuri jumped in: "Like if somebody just tells you one side of something. They're trying to get you to think a certain way."

"Yeah, some religions do that," Julian added.

"So what does that have to do with the issues we've been talking about?" I asked.

"You've been indoctrinating us!" someone yelled. A joke? I wasn't sure.

"Maybe," I said. "Maybe I have."

"Nah, you don't just show us one side," came a quick response.

"Are you sure?" I paused. "How do you know?"

I explained to the class that I'd posted a few of their comments about the grand jury's decision on Twitter and that someone responded by accusing me of biased teaching about the killings of Eric Garner and Michael Brown. I projected my Twitter feed and slowly scrolled through the conversation as I read the comments aloud. When I got to D.B.'s "You should stick to teaching recess on the playgrounds. Stay out of classrooms," the class exploded in laughter.

"Oooh, you got treated, Mr. Michie!"

After we'd read through the entire thread and talked about what D.B.'s main criticisms were, I told the class I thought the issue he'd raised was an important one.

"But he's being bogus, though," Noemi said.

"Okay, but I still want you to consider his point," I said. "Am I educating you or indoctrinating you? And how do you feel about it either way?" I moved toward the door. "I want you to talk about that for a few minutes. I'll be out in the hall. Yuri, you facilitate." I left and closed the door behind me.

I hoped that leaving the classroom would allow them to assess my teaching more freely. But even with me stationed in the hallway out of earshot, the activity was full of built-in bias. I'd been these kids' social studies teacher for nearly a semester, and with many I'd developed at least some level of trust and mutual affection. A few of them I'd known since they were 5th graders. Because of this, I knew they might feel the need to defend me against the accusations of some random guy on Twitter, which in turn would cloud their ability to consider the question without prejudice.

Still, I thought it was important to have them wrestle with it. We routinely looked for bias in almost any text we used in class—an interview, an online news report, a primary source—so why not give similar scrutiny to my curricular and pedagogical choices? After all, even though I knew where I stood on the issue, it was still something that gnawed at me at times: Was I exposing students to alternative viewpoints? Was I providing them with enough information to make informed judgments? Was I steering their thinking too heavily in a single direction?

I want my teaching to provide space for students to figure out what they think about the issues at hand. It's never been my intent to influence kids to blindly follow my lead. But I'd decided years earlier that the approach some teachers view as the antidote to "biased" instruction—being "unbiased" or not taking sides in the classroom—was not only misguided, it was impossible. Despite efforts to be impartial, teachers bring a worldview and a lifetime of experiences with them that influence what they teach—and, maybe even more importantly, what they don't. A teacher who designs lessons for 7th graders about the Industrial Revolution or famous inventors, but not about the Dawes Act or the routine lynchings of Black Americans, is doing more than making simple choices. At best, he's making a value judgment about which are more important; at worst, he's whitewashing history. It's a bias. It's taking sides.

Neutrality is often held up as the ideal for teachers—especially in subject areas like social studies, civics, or science. But the late historian Howard Zinn, author of *You Can't Be Neutral on a Moving Train*, argued in a 2005 interview that both educators and students should reject notions of assumed objectivity:

> [T]he world is already moving in certain directions. Wars are going on. Children are starving. And to be neutral, to pretend to neutrality, to not take a stand in a situation like that is to collaborate with whatever is going on, to allow it to happen. [As a teacher], I did not want to be a collaborator with what was happening. I wanted to enter into history. I wanted to play a role. I wanted my students to play a role. I wanted to intercede.[5]

So, in the current moment—when unarmed Black people are routinely killed by police, when the U.S. president orders the separation of immigrant children from their parents at the border, when the profits of corporations are valued more than the health of our planet—teachers can take one of four paths. We can avoid these topics altogether. We can, in the name of being impartial, simply "present information" about them. We can encourage students to use evidence and reasoning to determine their own positions on issues, while not revealing our own. Or we can, in the course of helping students deepen their own understandings, let them know where we stand, and why. I choose option D.

This doesn't mean I inundate students with one-sided lessons and fiery diatribes. Refusing to be neutral and engaging in indoctrination are not the same thing. When I teach about historical conflicts between Native people and the U.S. government, for example, I have students read primary sources that express different points of view. I try to help them dig deep to understand the assumptions behind federal policies and the impacts and limits of resistance to those policies. But I don't feign impartiality. I don't give moral equivalency to the Cherokee's right to remain on their land and the White power structure's covetous desire to take it away. We don't engage in debates about whether the forced assimilation of Native children in government-run boarding schools was a good idea. It wasn't.

Too often, social studies curriculum in schools serves as a cheerleading squad for oppressive governmental actions, for powerful interests, for the dominant White culture. In my classroom I aim to challenge that. I'm mostly at peace with letting students know I'm a concerned citizen, not a passive observer, and with being transparent about sharing my views. But I don't want them to feel pressured to adopt my way of thinking or to be fearful of taking quite different positions on the issues—and I try my best to be clear about that, too. Like so much of teaching, it can be a tricky balancing act, and at times I'm left second-guessing myself. Which is probably why D.B.'s pushback on Twitter touched a nerve in the first place.

* * *

When I stepped back into the classroom after my self-imposed hallway exile, my students, perhaps not surprisingly, exonerated me: I hadn't, they decided, tried to indoctrinate them. I told them I was grateful but that they were a tainted jury. They didn't let me off the hook completely, though. Several said they could often guess what I thought about an issue, even if I didn't state it directly, by my tone or energy level. One student said she could infer my point of view by the posters I displayed in my classroom.

But those who spoke up also said that these things didn't really bother them. What irritated them most about D.B.'s accusations, they said, had nothing to do with me. It was that he was giving them no credit, belittling their ability to think and reason for themselves.

"It's like he thinks we're stupid," Cristiano said. "Like we're gonna think one way just because you tell us something."

"People think just because we're kids we don't understand things," Yuri added. "But we do."

That night, before going to bed, I checked Twitter. I wondered if D.B. had snuck in another dig at me during the day. Instead, I saw a tweet directed at D.B. from Raul, a student whose attention I'd thought was drifting during the lesson. I didn't even know he was on Twitter.

"Why are you calling my teacher a liar?" it read. "I know what I saw on the video. You dont know what your talking about."

I scrolled through Raul's feed. He had also posted an article about Eric Garner's children's response to the grand jury decision and another about the impact of racism on people's mental and physical health.

I wasn't sure how to feel. Should I be encouraged that he was doing further exploration of the issue outside of the classroom and passing on articles to others? Should I be concerned that he was being unduly influenced by my teaching? Should I be gratified that he felt the need to come to my defense?

The next morning at school, I would tell Raul I was proud of him for doing additional reading on his own. I would thank him for having my back. I would assure him that, in the future, I could handle the Twitter attacks myself. At that moment, though, I just smiled.

* * *

As the school year wore on—and *wore on* does seem like the right phrase for that year—we would come to know additional names of Black people killed by police or who died while in police custody. John Crawford. Tamir Rice. Freddie Gray. Sandra Bland. When Walter Scott was killed by a police officer in South Carolina that April, I first heard about it the following morning from a concerned 7th grader.

In March, the U.S. Department of Justice released two reports related to the shooting death of Michael Brown.[6] The first, which was based on interviews with witnesses as well as crime scene evidence, concluded that the actions of Darren Wilson, the officer who killed Michael Brown, did not rise to "prosecutable violations." His use of deadly force, the report said, was not in violation of Fourth Amendment protections guaranteed by the U.S. Constitution. The second report, which focused more broadly on practices of the Ferguson Police Department as a whole, identified long-standing patterns of racial bias and discrimination by police against the city's Black residents. According to then attorney general Eric Holder, "Ferguson police officers routinely violate[d] the Fourth Amendment in stopping people without reasonable suspicion, arresting them without probable cause, and using unreasonable force against them."[7]

After reading the reports, I wasn't sure how my students would respond. Part of me wondered whether I had made a mistake by jumping into the unit headlong to start the year, if I had been in too much of a hurry to teach about something that still had so many unknowns. Teacher Matthew Kay, in his book *Not Light, but Fire: How to Lead Meaningful Race Conversations in the Classroom*,[8] offers a word of caution in this regard. "Just because a controversy is outside making a fuss doesn't mean we have to open the [classroom] doors to it," Kay writes. "When we're at our best, we ignore its noise, size it up, judge whether it should be admitted as is—or if it needs to go home and change." The only measure of cover Kay provides me is in his next line: "This discernment challenge is hardest in turbulent times."[9]

Those times were, without a doubt, turbulent ones. Looking back, I wouldn't change my decision to take on the unit. I still believe my original impulse—that the issue was too important not to teach, and that it deserved not a one-off lesson, but an extended study—was a sound one. As Kay acknowledges, "[o]ccasionally, a moment's urgency is real, and not just a by-product of a teacher's impatience."[10] For me, the killing of Michael Brown, and the larger issues it came to represent, was one of those moments. If I could go back in time, I would certainly do some things differently. But that's often the case in teaching. We do our best and then learn from our mistakes.

A couple days after the Justice Department's findings were released, I presented a summary of the two reports to my students. I explained that their investigation showed a history of racism toward Black residents on the part of the Ferguson Police Department but had not found evidence that Darren Wilson violated federal civil rights laws when he shot and killed Michael Brown. Some students were confused. ("What about the witnesses who said he had his hands up?") Others were angry. ("But he still didn't have to shoot him six times. That's still wrong.") Still others seemed resigned to early-onset cynicism. ("The cop's always gonna be right. Don't matter.") I tried to explain the difference between state criminal statutes and federal civil rights law, and how that impacted the findings. But I sensed that many of the kids' minds were not on those details—at least not yet. They were thinking about Michael Brown. He was, after all, a teen like them, and they'd long ago recognized that his life mattered.

CHAPTER NINE

Stupidity and Evaluation

During my second year as a teacher in the early 1990s, my sister, Lynn, visited Chicago for a few days and spent an afternoon in my classroom. At the time I was teaching small groups of 6th graders—and one group of 2nd graders—in a converted coat closet, which was jammed to capacity with just seven students, eight desks, and me. We managed to squeeze in an extra chair for Lynn, who at the time was studying to be a minister, in the open doorway.

At the end of the day, after the students had been dismissed, I asked Lynn for her thoughts on the two classes she had observed.

She paused for a moment. "The girls didn't say very much," she said.

"Hmm," was about all I managed to get out. "I hadn't noticed that."

The specificity of her observation took me aback—mainly because the specific thing she had observed hadn't even occurred to me. I suppose I'd been expecting something vaguely positive like, "It was fun" or "The kids were great."

What had stood out to Lynn was that the boys dominated discussions while the girls stayed mostly silent. I'd thought the classes had gone okay, and I'd completely missed the dynamic she had seen so clearly. But as I thought about it over the next few days, I realized that it hadn't been a fluke. The boys did take up most of air in that tiny closet. It was an ah-ha moment for me, and from that point on, I was much more awake to the ways gender played out in my classroom. My sister's informal evaluation that day—really just careful observation followed by helpful comments—ended up having a lasting impact on my teaching.

Having your teaching observed by another adult was rare back then, unless you had a teacher's aide or a team-teaching situation. I remember being observed formally by my principal only two times during my first 9 years in the classroom. In those days, teacher evaluation seemed to be more of a divination process, consisting of an administrator's general perception of you as a teacher: what they sensed through interactions or intuition—or, in some cases, simply on whether they liked you or not.

But despite that, each spring every teacher in CPS found an envelope in her school mailbox with a single page folded inside. On the paper was a brief checklist of "strengths" and "weaknesses," and toward the bottom a blank space where the principal inked in the teacher's annual rating. Most teachers, myself included, unfolded the paper year after year to see the word "Superior" written in the blank. It was the best you could do, the highest rating on the mysterious scale, and it wasn't hard to get. "Superiors" were doled out so routinely that I once overheard a teacher bemoaning what she considered to be an unfair rating of "Excellent." I recall talking with teacher-friends in those days about how loose the evaluation process seemed, how infrequently we got observed, and how a "superior" rating meant nothing if almost everybody got one. "Shouldn't we have a better system?" I wondered aloud.

By the time I returned to teaching in 2012, a new system was in place. Whether it was better was another matter.

* * *

Sometime in late spring of my first year back, my 8th graders' conversation veered from the documentary film we were discussing to the topic of standardized testing. I don't remember how it came up exactly, but if you're a teacher or student in a Chicago school, testing of some sort is always lurking just over your shoulder.

"The NWEA test doesn't even test us on what we're actually learning in class," Jesus protested. After a couple of other students agreed, I told them that their scores on the NWEA MAP—a computer-based test known more formally as the Northwest Evaluation Association's Measures of Academic Progress—would nonetheless be used to grade their teachers as part of Chicago Public Schools' new "value-added" system of evaluation.

"But wait, what if you don't teach reading or math?" Briana asked, aware that CPS only used the NWEA to assess those two subjects.

"Then they base your evaluation on the average reading scores of the entire school," I said. "That's how I'll be evaluated." Around the room, faces twisted in confusion.

"But you don't even teach reading!" Briana said. And then several, almost in unison: "That's stupid!" Leave it to young people to see through the insanity of education policy in a matter of minutes.

My 8th graders' blunt analysis that day reminded me of Herb Kohl's prescient 2003 book, *Stupidity and Tears: Teaching and Learning in Troubled Times.*[1] The stupidity in Kohl's title referred to education policies that were then just kicking into high gear—policies that valued compliance over creativity, sapped the joy from classrooms, and had "the consequence of perpetuating ignorance, keeping poor, defiant, marginalized youth 'in their place.'"[2] The tears were the by-product of such policies: those of teachers following ridiculous mandates against their better judgment or of students subjected to the constraints of a scripted, seemingly irrelevant curriculum.

A decade later, things had only gotten stupider. The corporate education reform agenda, with its insistence that anything that counts can be counted, had ushered in a new era of data-driven initiatives. Hundreds of millions of dollars from the Bill & Melinda Gates Foundation, along with a shove from Barack Obama's Race to the Top initiative, pushed districts across the country to develop revamped teacher evaluation systems. The stated goal was to improve "teacher quality"—which would, it was hoped by the reformers, lead to the promised land of increased student achievement.

The embrace of value-added measures (VAMs) for purposes of teacher evaluation was one of the centerpieces of this shift. The complex statistical calculations used in value-added formulas were supposed to isolate a teacher's impact on his students' growth—as measured, of course, by gains on standardized test scores. But no convincing research indicated that value-added models provided reliable results. A statement on VAMs by the American Statistical Association noted that they "typically measure correlation, not causation" and added that VAM scores have large standard errors that "make rankings [of teachers] unstable, even under the best scenarios for modeling."[3]

Chicago Public Schools had just begun using VAM in 2012, the year I returned to the classroom, as part of a new teacher evaluation initiative. The system was created in response to an Illinois law, passed in 2010, that required all school districts in the state to use "student growth" as part of teacher evaluations.[4] I was fortunate that year to join a team of talented and experienced upper grade teachers at Quincy. Each of them, in my view, did extraordinary work with our kids. But when our initial VAM scores were released the next fall, they painted a far different picture.

All six of us—with nearly 100 years of experience in Chicago classrooms between us—had negative value-added scores. My own score was a -0.79. What that meant was that, according to the VAM calculations, each of us had made a *negative* difference in our students' growth compared to what an "average" teacher might have achieved. Put most simply, our students learned less because they had us as teachers.

Even if you know it's all a bunch of number-crunching craziness, even as you realize that the margin of error is almost the same size as your value-added rating, it's still demoralizing. And the assumptions that accompany VAM are maddening: That good teaching can be neatly and precisely quantified. That the depth and breadth of a teacher's work can be captured by student test scores. That a mathematical formula, no matter how complex, can grasp the impact of poverty or inadequate housing or exposure to gun violence on the educational life of a child.

The day after we received our value-added scores, I arrived at school nearly an hour early. One of my colleagues, Cudberto Esparza, was already in his classroom, as he always was, every morning without fail, ready to provide extra math tutoring for students who needed it. Sometimes one kid showed up; other days it was five or six. Each of them would gladly tell you how much value Mr. Esparza added to their lives. And they wouldn't need any convoluted calculations to do it.

* * *

In an effort to push back against the lunacy of VAM, the Chicago Teachers Union leadership negotiated with the Board of Education for a third component to be added to the equation of teacher ratings: subject- and grade-specific student performance tasks. These would be created by teachers and given twice a year—once at the beginning and once at the end—in order to demonstrate student growth in targeted disciplinary skills. In theory, this sounded like a positive development: home-grown rather than standardized, teacher-initiated rather than district-imposed, and performance-based rather than multiple choice. In practice, though, they provided little comfort. Responding to craziness can sometimes just multiply it.

One problem was that many students came to loathe the performance tasks. In the middle grades, some kids ended up having to complete a task in several different subject areas, which meant doing six or more of them over the course of the year—in addition to all the other standardized assessments they had to endure. Informing a class that they would have to complete a performance task was nearly always met with groans of anticipatory pain and a chorus of anguished cries: "Again?!"

Another issue was that some teachers used the performance tasks in an attempt to game the system, openly telling their students not to do their best on the beginning-of-the-year task in hopes of showing more growth by year's end. A similar strategy was to inform students that the initial task would not be graded, then switch gears and announce that the end-of-year task would go in the gradebook—again, in an effort to artificially inflate results. I heard about these practices anecdotally from students at a couple schools, so I have no idea how widespread either of them were. But in light of the pressurized atmosphere that had been created by high-stakes testing, it was hard to blame teachers for responding this way. Still, it turned the entire endeavor into little more than a time-consuming charade.

But one of the worst problems was that, at least in social studies, the tasks and rubrics themselves were sometimes of questionable value. One year, the task's final question—which counted for 60% of the total score—required students to write a short essay using at least three of the four provided historical documents to support their answer. Sounds reasonable–except that two of the four documents were clearly not trustworthy sources. So, in order to receive a top score, students would have to cite at least one unreliable source. What historian does that? It was a poorly constructed, insufficiently vetted question, and–at least from my perspective–invalidated the entire task.

I vented to colleagues about the performance tasks for several years, but I was too busy with my daily teaching responsibilities to do anything to challenge them. Then, one year, the combination of being perpetually overwhelmed and a habitual procrastinator led me to do by accident what I should have done in protest: I missed the deadline and failed to give the end-of-year assessment. I figured I would receive a score of zero for that portion (10%) of my evaluation, but I didn't think it would tank my overall rating, which had stayed the same no matter what mixture of numbers fed into the formula each year. According to CPS, I was consistently a "proficient" teacher. Not stellar; not bad. *Decent*, to use the favored vernacular of my students.

The next fall when I received my "Educator Evaluation Summary Report," though, things got weird. I noticed that not only did I have a score listed for the performance task–I had a perfect score: 100% of my students had made growth. It was by far the best I'd ever done. The only problem, of course, was that it was complete fiction. I'd never given the end-of-year task or submitted any scores.

Where had the numbers come from? I had no idea. I didn't have any friends at the district office. Nobody was watching my back.

It was all such a mess. So much time and energy and money devoted to erecting a supposedly cutting-edge system for evaluating teachers–one that would, with numerical precision, separate the distinguished from the proficient, the basic from the unsatisfactory. But from my front-row seat, it was mostly smoke and mirrors. Even worse, for me, was that neither VAM nor the performance tasks did what good evaluation should: help me improve my teaching, my daily work with kids.

* * *

"Hello, class! You all look ready to learn this afternoon!" It was the final period of the day, but I was all smiles and game-show-host energy.

"Thank you, Mr. Michie!" my students responded in sing-song unison.

One of our school's assistant principals was sitting at the rear of the classroom, ready to record evidence from my lesson that aligned with Charlotte Danielson's ubiquitous "Framework for Teaching."

"Who can tell me what we were studying yesterday?" I asked.

Nearly 30 hands shot up around the room.

"We were learning about presidential campaign commercials!" Sofie gushed. "I love learning about that!"

"Fantastic, Sofie. So, today–"

Nova interrupted: "Mr. Michie, can I pass out the handouts?"

"Sure! I'd forgotten all about that. Thanks for taking initiative!"

"You're such a good helper, Nova," Kasandra said.

"She, sure is! Now, is everybody ready to learn?" I asked with a peppiness usually reserved for hokey teacher-training videos.

"Yes!" the kids shouted as one.

It was as if they'd rehearsed it. And they had.

I'd enlisted my homeroom students to be part of the short skit as a lighthearted way to begin my formal observation–a cheesy parody of a "perfect" lesson. My assistant principal had observed me enough in the past to know within the first few seconds that the scene playing out before her was fraudulent, and she had a laugh as we transitioned from the fake lesson into a real one. That is, as "real" as an observed lesson can be. When evaluators are sitting in your classroom with their laptops or notepads at the ready, what transpires between teacher and students is always at least a bit performative–though neither the observed nor the observer is usually eager to admit it.

Like everything else related to teacher evaluation in Chicago schools, lesson observations had undergone a major overhaul since the 1990s. Gone were the days of getting formally observed only in presidential election years. Gone, too, were "superior" ratings based on ghost evidence. In their place, for new teachers, were four observations each year–three formal, one informal–with each of the formal observations accompanied by a pre- and post-observation conference. For most of my observations during the first few years of my return, I had not one, not two, but three administrators watching me and taking copious notes on their MacBooks. Afterward, they collaborated to fill out a detailed report based on the Danielson framework, and I received numerical ratings on a scale of one to four in each of 15 subcategories.

I know, I know. Be careful what you ask for.

It was a drastic change, and I had little interest in the quantitative piece. But I did think classroom observations—and follow-up reflective discussions between administrators and educators—had the potential to help teachers improve. With each new school year, each new class, each unique and idiosyncratic young person who comes through the door, fresh challenges present themselves. Good teachers realize that their work must evolve, that they are always in the process of learning, of becoming. Besides, coming back to work with middle schoolers after so many years away, I was filled with doubt—not bluster. I knew I needed to get better as a teacher, and I realized I probably had blind spots I hadn't even considered. Observations, from my perspective, were—or at least could be—a useful tool.

And for the most part, for me, they were. Our principal and her two assistants were careful observers and took their roles as evaluators seriously. They also had an important advantage: all three had been teachers at Quincy for years before becoming administrators. They knew the kids, the parents, and the neighborhood well. With the rise of principal training programs that attract "talent" from the corporate realm, this was increasingly rare. And it mattered. When I got observed, I didn't get the feeling my administrators were just checking off attributes they'd been told were important in a principal preparation course. They were connecting what they witnessed to a wealth of accumulated knowledge—about good teaching, the school's community context, and the children in front of them. So, while I didn't exactly look forward to being observed, it also wasn't something I dreaded.

I realized, though, that my ambivalent attitude toward observations wasn't shared by all. New teachers were often anxious about them, and even some CPS veterans I knew thought their administrators' classroom visits were more punitive than helpful. Despite the new evaluation rubric's veneer of numerical objectivity, vindictive principals could still use it as a bludgeon. On a listserve I subscribed to, a veteran Chicago teacher complained of being targeted for low evaluations so her school could bring in a new—and much less expensive—teacher. On Twitter, I'd read accounts from a number of educators—many of whom are of color—whose principals had evaluated them poorly in retaliation for their outspoken critiques or advocacy work. When observations are weaponized in this manner, it sends a clear message to other teachers: don't challenge leadership, keep your head down, stay quiet, and hope for the best. So, while observations have the potential to help teachers improve, they can only work as part of teacher evaluations when undertaken in good faith by fair and thoughtful administrators.

* * *

Has teacher evaluation in CPS gotten better since the 1990s? The short answer is yes. Any system is better than no system at all, which is essentially what was in place back then. But the new, data-drenched approach embraced by the district is not nearly as accurate or as useful as its proponents like to believe. Although regular classroom observations and the conversations that flow from them can be useful in the right hands, too much of the rest, when examined honestly, has little real meaning.

On the surface, it has a certain deceptive appeal. The focus on numbers, on quantification, on a "bottom line" seems to simplify and make compliant what is, in reality, a complex and unruly endeavor. But unlike earnings reports or year-over-year sales figures, teaching and learning can't be reduced to mere data points. Even if the numbers were, in some imaginary world, shown to be precise and reliable, they would still only reflect a small portion of what good teaching is or should be. What about the democratic ideal or community involvement? What about creating antiracist and antibias curriculum? What about centering student voice, relationship-building, arts integration, youth organizing, and supporting former students after they've graduated? Pseudoscientific measurements just can't provide a meaningful way to assess the multiplicities of a teacher's work with young people.

I've been in the midst of the data churn for several years now, and I'm still not a believer. Remember the 100% growth I showed on the performance task I never gave? I'd assumed it was just a fluke, a one-time glitch. But the next year something similar happened. I received a value-added score—and a pretty good one, at that—for a reading class I never taught. Yet combined with my observation score, it gave me a final rating that, for the first time ever, barely bumped me into the "distinguished" category—the supposed cream of the crop of Chicago public school teachers.

Just another day in the land of make-believe. Forgive me for not celebrating.

CHAPTER TEN

Unfolding Hope

As I returned to my classroom in January 2017 after a much-needed winter break, part of me was hoping to leave Donald Trump—and much of 2016, really—behind. Sure, I knew he would be inaugurated soon. I knew his already ubiquitous presence would become even more suffocating. And I feared his frightening campaign promises would soon begin to land brutally on people's lives—including the lives of my students. But he had already wormed his way into so many of our lessons over the past year that I thought we were ready, at least for a while, to turn to other topics, other themes.

I should've known better. By the end of his first week in office, Trump had already signed an Executive Order to begin building a wall along the Mexican border, threatened to "send in the Feds" if Chicago's gun violence numbers didn't improve, blocked Syrian refugees from entering the United States, and temporarily banned immigration from seven majority Muslim countries. It was impossible for us to ignore him.

For my students—mostly children or grandchildren of immigrants from Mexico, along with a few Central American and Muslim immigrants—the worries that accompanied Trump's flurry of first-week actions were not new. Throughout 2016, as the bizarre presidential election and the spiraling levels of gun violence in some of Chicago's most forgotten communities made headlines, my students never had the luxury granted to most White Americans, who looked on from a comfortable distance. For the kids I teach, it all played out—literally—close to home, and the accompanying loss and fear were visceral, palpable.

* * *

As 2016 began, late-night talk shows and social media were still having plenty of fun with the notion of a Trump presidency. But my students were already worried. The possibility of Trump landing in the White House had never felt like a joke to them, and as months went by, their concerns grew. They listened as he categorically disparaged Mexicans and Muslims, as he threatened to end birthright citizenship, as he demonized Black and brown Chicago, as he repeatedly promised to build a wall. To my students, these were neither throwaway stump-speech lines nor laughable proposals. They were direct threats.

"Mr. Michie," a 7th grader with special needs wondered aloud in class. "If Donald Trump wins and my mom gets deported, can I come live with you and your family?"

"I don't think that's gonna happen," I said. "If it does, though, we'll figure something out. You're gonna be okay. Don't worry."

But he did worry. Despite the reassurances of teachers, despite all the polls, despite the many prognosticators predicting a Hillary Clinton victory, he was fearful, as were many of my students, of what might be. But they were also afraid of what had been, of what already was.

On a Monday evening in early May, I got a text from Carlos, a former student: "Hey Mr. Michie I don't know if you had heard they just shot Leo the 7th grader." *No,* I thought. *Please, no.* I put my phone down and stared at the display. I felt numb. Leo was in my homeroom—a bright, often quiet kid who loved playing basketball in the park, reading realistic fiction, and making his classmates laugh. Earlier that day, we'd stood back to back in the hallway to see who was taller. I still had him by a half inch. "I bet you'll pass me by the end of the year," I'd said.

Let him be okay. Let him be okay.

A few minutes later, another text from Carlos: "Mr. Michie he passed away. They just texted me right now telling me that he didn't pull through." I spent the rest of that evening in a fog of tears and memories, texting back and forth with students, colleagues, and my principal, who had gone to the hospital as soon as she'd heard to be with Leo's family. It didn't seem possible that it was really happening.

I had been to the funerals of several former students over the years. But I'd never had a current student killed, never had to face all his friends in class the next morning. I wasn't sure what to say, what to do, how to proceed. I knew information traveled fast in the neighborhood—it always had, even before Facebook or texting—so it never occurred to me that I'd be the one to break the news to any of my students. But when one boy ambled in, hair tousled as if he'd woken up 10 minutes earlier, I could tell by the way he looked around at the awkward stillness of his classmates that he had no inkling. Telling him was one of the toughest things I've had to do in all my years as a teacher.

My colleagues and I decided to let all the 7th and 8th graders spend the entire morning out in the hallway. We hugged. We cried. We stood around in clusters, speaking in whispers, still stunned. Later, my homeroom students gathered chairs in a circle and shared. We meditated, as we do every day. And we created a community memorial to Leo in the hallway, with photos, drawings, poems, and remembrances.

The week after Leo was killed, a class of 2nd graders—along with their teacher, Erika Gomez, who grew up in Back of the Yards and attended our school as a student—slowly filed into our classroom in the middle of a social studies lesson. My students watched, confused. "What are they doing?" one student asked aloud. When the last of the children had taken their places in a semicircle that embraced the older students, three stepped forward.

"We know you are really sad about your friend, Leonardo," a girl said.

"But we want you to know that there is hope. Don't lose hope," another added. "So we made little presents for you to keep and to know that life goes on."

For the next few minutes, the 2nd graders made their way around the room, handing out cards they'd made for the teens. "I'm sorry for your loss," one chubby-cheeked boy said. Near him, a pair of girls hugged as tears rolled down the 8th grader's cheeks. She wiped them away, smiled, and gave her card-bearer another tight squeeze.

It had been an unimaginably difficult 2 weeks, and the surprise visit had come at just the right time. At some point, we'd need to continue thinking about the root causes of violence in the neighborhood, about what the city needed to do to support young people in communities like ours, about our own roles in helping to bring about change.

But at that moment, we needed to remember Leo. We needed to hold on to each other. We needed just what those 2nd graders provided.

* * *

That any school-based learning can happen when kids are experiencing such emotional upheaval, such an avalanche of sadness and fear, is something akin to a miracle. But it does. Young people are resilient—far more than they should have to be—and we do our best to move forward. As in many middle school classrooms, my students that year were by turns deeply engaged, flat-out bored, lost in reflection, or writhing in uproarious laughter. They wrote poems and read novels and explored big questions like "What is the meaning of patriotism?" and "What is the role of the media in a democracy?" They learned.

In October, in the midst of a unit on the presidential election, my social studies classes watched Khizr Khan's speech from the Democratic convention. Almost none of them had seen it before, and when Khan pulled a slim booklet out of his jacket pocket and said to the camera, "Donald Trump . . . let me ask you: Have you even read the United States Constitution? I will gladly lend you my copy,"[1] their roar of applause seemed to shake the walls. One girl turned to me and said, "That right there gave me chills."

The morning after the election, the electricity generated by the Khan video seemed like a distant memory. Like much of America, many of my students believed that Hillary Clinton would win. Or maybe they just wanted to believe it. Most of them weren't huge Clinton fans (many had favored Bernie Sanders during the primary season), but Trump was frightening. When I asked if anybody wanted to share how they were feeling in the wake of the results, few did. So, I asked each student to give me just one word. *Worried*, *afraid*, and *disappointed* came up often. Later in the period, when we looked at the exit polls broken down by race, it was no surprise who had disappointed them. Trump had won only the White vote, while losing in a landslide among every other racial demographic.

My students are not naïve. I don't think they look to electoral politics as a simple balm for their hurts or struggles. They are keen observers of current events and history, and are quick to detect injustices perpetrated by those in power, whether we're discussing Jim Crow laws or the cover-up of the Laquan McDonald killing in Chicago. But they are also, on the whole, not jaded. Although they note the hypocrisies, and live out the stark differences between the America of textbook mythology and the America of their backyard, many want to believe that the country's people will, when it really matters, do right by them. In that sense, the presidential election was another crushing loss in a year of crushing losses.

As painful as Leo's death had been, it wasn't the first, or last, to shake our school's community during that year. Sidewalk altars became a recurring feature of the neighborhood landscape, their wilting flowers and Virgen de Guadalupe prayer candles serving as reminders of the fragility of life for kids who walked past each day. Two of those killed were older brothers of one of our 8th graders. Five had once been students at our school. The oldest among them was just 22.

So, were they gang members? I can almost see that question bubbling to the surface in the minds of some readers. My short answer is that it doesn't matter. They were young—most of them still teens—and now they are gone. Asking if they were gang members seems little more than a pretext for concluding their deaths were justified or at least undeserving of sympathy. It's the same line of thinking, in reverse, that prompts journalists to alert readers that a murdered teen was an "honor student"—as if a kid who failed a class or had a "C" average is somehow expendable. Of the young people our school's community lost that year, some were gang-affiliated. Others, like Leo, were not. Either way, the questions we should ask in the wake of such violence are deeper ones: Why do so many Black and Latino young men feel a sense of hopelessness or despair? What can schools do to better embrace and connect with kids on the margins? Where are the job opportunities and mental health supports for young people in our city's neediest neighborhoods?

Asking good questions is, of course, part of the territory for teachers. But for me, the best, most urgent question of the year was not part of any unit plan or asked by any adult at our school. It was posed by an 8th grader, toward the end of an assembly that addressed the violence in our community, how it was affecting us, and how we might respond. The girl who asked it raised her hand tentatively before saying, "How does hope unfold?"

The philosophical turn of the question, as well as its somewhat unusual construction, seemed to take everyone by surprise. If anyone responded, I don't remember what they said. But the question stuck with me over the course of the year: *How does hope unfold?* The image it brought to mind, for me at least, was of hope as a process, a series of actions, that build on one another over time. It resonated with me in ways that similar questions, such as "Where do we find hope?" do not.

For many educators, the answer to that last question—Where do we find hope?—is often simple and obvious: the kids. We find hope in our students, the next generation. It's a cliché of sorts, but I've said it myself, many times, and there is truth to be found in the words. Still, the events of that year pushed me to reconsider that response, to wonder if it is, in some ways, a cop-out for adults, a way to place a weight onto the shoulders of young people who shouldn't have to carry it.

That thought was echoed by one of my 8th-grade students, Yuri, who closed a poem at our Spoken Word night with these words:

> They tell me to have hope, that everything is going to be okay.
> But how can I believe them?
> How can I convince myself that everything's gon' be alright?
> How can you ask me to have hope when bodies are being
> dropped day after day? . . .
> If there is a way to get hope,
> teach me,
> teach us.

That, in turn, may be too formidable a load for teachers to bear alone. In times of tragedy, we all flail about, full of uncertainty, unsure of how to respond. But sometimes what children need, psychologist

Jason Thompson says, is for us to be "empathic witnesses" to their suffering and loss.[2] The only real way forward, it seems, is to trudge through the pain hand in hand.

And that we continued to do. Teachers instituted talking circles in their classrooms. Our school administration set aside money for therapists to support students' emotional health and devoted an entire professional development session to teacher wellness. In late November, in response to the election results, a number of students and teachers participated in a "We Belong" unity march and rally, where one of our 8th graders delivered a powerful speech in support of her undocumented brother.

Outside the school's walls, the neighborhood was, as always, full of beautiful people and fierce love. Gun violence and gangs do not define it. Kids played soccer at the park. Some went to confirmation classes or played in a marimba ensemble at the local parish. Mothers led parenting classes. First-generation college students gathered for support sessions. A weekly Reflections group drew 15 or so young men who met to discuss their struggles and ways to address them.

And in the classroom, we did our best to keep going, to keep living. We began our meditation every day by remembering Leo. We explored the historical oppression of Native people by the U.S. government and the lessons we might learn from their resistance. We read the words of heroic Americans like Ida B. Wells and Malcolm X, and analyzed their meaning for the struggles of today. The path ahead was still dusted over with painful memories and apprehension about the future, but the challenge was clear: Day by day, piece by piece, unfold hope. Together.

CHAPTER ELEVEN

What Manny Taught Me

In May 2017, then secretary of state Rex Tillerson held a "town hall" about translating Donald Trump's "America First" slogan into foreign policy. One of the key points of his talk was that U.S. economic and national security interests must take precedence over long-held democratic principles. "Our values around freedom, human dignity, the way people are treated—those are our values," Tillerson said. "Those are not our policies."[1]

On one level, there was nothing remarkable about Tillerson's comments. The U.S. government has, after all, regularly tossed aside its values throughout the decades in the name of financial gain, strategic advantage, and the maintenance of global dominance and White supremacy. As one of my students put it, "They say they about freedom and justice, but they ain't really about that." The only surprise, really, was that Tillerson would articulate the duplicitous stance so openly.

Like government officials, educators are skilled at using lofty language, often in the form of catch phrases, to talk about our beliefs and values. We're teaching "the whole child" and preparing "lifelong learners." We're helping students build "21st-century skills" through "individualized instruction." We're creating "inclusive communities" that always—*always*—put "children first." Except when we're not, which is more often than most of us would like to admit. Yet we're not always eager to examine the hypocrisy.

The problem is not the inflated language. We should have high expectations for ourselves and the kids we teach, and it can help to have aspirational words to guide us. But when they are repeated so often, regurgitated like food scraps in a clogged drain, they can easily become empty phrases, signifying big ideals but meaning nothing.

Is our instruction really individualized? How so? And if it is, why is the entire class always reading the same story or demonstrating their learning in the same way? Is our school community truly inclusive? How do we know? Why are so many Black kids being singled out as discipline problems? Or why, in a mostly Latinx school, do so few White teachers speak Spanish? It's one thing to toss around clichés about the kind of education we believe young people deserve; bringing it to life, day in and day out, over the course of an entire school year, is another matter altogether.

My own classroom is a prime example. If you came by unannounced for a random visit, you might see 8th graders presenting about LGBTQ advocacy, or taping an original podcast about a parent who is in prison, or preparing for a mock trail centering on First Amendment rights. But depending on the day or the hour, you might instead see students answering multiple-choice questions or me struggling to get through an uninspired lesson; them losing focus or me losing my patience. These are not everyday occurrences, and they are not my proudest moments as a teacher. But they happen.

Unlike Tillerson, though, I'm not content with the contradictions between my beliefs and my actions. They bother me. I'm not okay with saying, "This is what I'm about as a teacher: seeing each student as fully human, creating a challenging yet affirming space, and centering issues of equity and justice. But those are my values—not my practices." One of the main things that keeps me energized is a continual striving to close the gap between the classroom I envision for my students and the one that actually plays out.

But I still lapse into moments, or sometimes entire lessons, of misguided choices and bad teaching. Like the time Manny set me straight.

* * *

I was never sure which Manny would walk into my class on a given day. Most of the time, he was wired: buzzing with energy, moving about the room constantly, blurting out answers or off-the-wall comments. Other days, he was unplugged: head down on the desk, withdrawn, barely saying a word. Either way, he could be difficult to keep focused.

Manny loved classic Mexican music and spending hours on YouTube. A member of the school's track team, he was lightning fast, and on the days they practiced inside (a common occurrence in Chicago schools with no access to proper facilities), I remember seeing him zoom past the open door of my classroom every few minutes, a blur of joyous athleticism.

One day, after spending nearly a week studying European governments' responses to the stream of Syrian and northern African refugees at their borders, I engaged Manny's class in a couple lessons centered on political cartoons about the topic. Political cartoons can be useful teaching tools, especially for kids who struggle with written texts. Their single-panel layouts and stark visuals help make complex ideas more understandable for English language learners and those with special needs. And they allow students to synthesize their learning about a topic while honing their inferencing and analysis skills.

After an introductory lesson that reviewed common techniques used by political cartoonists—symbolism, exaggeration, irony—groups of students selected a single cartoon to analyze based on four questions:

- What do you see? What's happening in the cartoon?
- What is the artist's point of view? How do you know?
- How are symbolism, exaggeration, and/or irony being used?
- Do you agree or disagree with their point of view, and why?

Twenty minutes later, each group took turns discussing their cartoon in front of the class. Students questioned their peers' analyses, pointed out details the presenters had missed, or offered up alternative interpretations. They had a lot to say—which showed me how much they'd learned about the topic. So, when the groups were finished, I said I'd take volunteers to do a few more. Instead of preparing their thoughts in advance, though, they'd analyze them on the fly, in real time. This excited about a third of the class—those who relished speaking in front of others—and horrified most of the rest, who were doing their best to become invisible. Manny, who had come in energized and had been vocal throughout, was one of the first to volunteer.

He and three other students examined a cartoon showing a raft of refugees approaching a shoreline. An elephant dressed in a suit stands on dry land, whispering to a man whose hat is labeled *Europe*. "My advice?" the elephant says. "Build a wall." Each of the four student volunteers was supposed to answer only one of the questions, but Manny dominated the discussion, interrupting to add his take several times. Still, he was enjoying the spotlight, and his comments on the cartoon were spot on.

"Okay, good job, everybody. We have time for one more group. Who wants to go up?"

As the other three students returned to their seats, Manny's hand shot in the air. "I wanna go again! I wanna do another one!"

I ignored him and searched for other hands. I called three students up to the stools where the panel had been sitting.

"Mr. Michie! Mr. Michie!" Manny called out, not yet giving up his spot. "Let me do another one!" He was holding on to the edges of the stool, bobbing up and down like a rocket about to take off.

"Manny, go sit down. We have to give everybody a chance."

"But they don't wanna do it! Look!"

He was right. No other hands were up. "One more," I said. "Come on—Bianca? Ricardo?"

I waited for another volunteer. By this time, the class had begun to get restless. Conversations were bubbling up. Behind me, Manny's voice was insistent and unceasing. "Mr. Michie, Mr. Michie!"

I held out.

"C'mon, Mr. Michie! I wanna go again!"

I scanned the room once more.

Still, Manny's voice behind me: "Lemme go! Mr. Michie, I wanna do it!"

I turned to him, voice raised. "Manny—if you don't quiet down and go back to your seat you're gonna lose all the points you just got for doing this!"

Manny didn't miss a beat. "I don't care about the points!" he said almost gleefully. "I just wanna participate!"

In that moment, everything screeched to a stop. Manny's words froze me. I felt like a politician caught in a lie on live TV. A flood of thoughts rushed through my head in just a few seconds. I wasn't sure exactly what I wanted to say, but I knew I didn't want to let the moment pass without comment.

"All right, listen up," I said. A few conversations continued. "Listen, everybody–please. I need to explain something."

It got quiet.

"What I just said to Manny–that I was going to take his points away if he didn't sit down–that was a really horrible thing to say."

A few kids giggled.

"No, I'm serious. I don't even know where it came from. It's probably something one of my teachers used to say when I was a kid. But it goes against everything I believe. And what Manny just said–when he said he didn't care about the points, that he just wanted to participate–that's *exactly* what I believe about education. It's not about the points. It's not about the grades. It's about learning, about thinking, about being engaged. About the things you were all doing today."

I looked at Manny. He was checking out the reaction of his classmates, maybe unsure of how to take this all in. His slight grin looked half-embarrassed, half-self-satisfied.

"Anyway, I'm sorry," I said. "I shouldn't have said it. That's not the kind of teacher I want to be."

"It's okay, Mr. Michie," Martha said. "It's not that big of a deal."

"Yeah, we'll forgive you," Jose deadpanned. "Just give us some extra points."

Then the group at the front of the class proceeded to analyze the final cartoon–with Manny's unbridled exuberance still on full display.

* * *

The "philosophy of education" essay is a cornerstone assignment for many college students studying to become teachers. It's typically pitched as an attempt to synthesize what they've learned from classic theorists like John Dewey and Maria Montessori, or more contemporary education writers like Angela Valenzuela and Chris Emdin, into their own manifesto about teaching and learning. During the years I taught preservice teachers, my students often grumbled about the assignment, and I could understand why: weighty ideas and sweeping statements can seem far removed from the hundreds of tiny moments and split-second decisions that make up a day in the life of a classroom.

But in my experience, it is exactly these moments and decisions where it is most crucial to be clear about one's beliefs. If not, it's easy to get caught up in the undertow of schooling-as-usual, to go along with senseless practices or harmful policies instead of asking why, to respond expediently rather than thoughtfully, to be slowly pulled away from the kind of classroom you'd once imagined.

This can happen to any teacher in any setting, but the danger is even greater in struggling city schools, where the overlapping impacts of poverty and segregation on students' lives can lead educators—especially White educators—to end up sounding a lot like Rex Tillerson: "Oh, I love inquiry learning and peer mediation—they're great. But they won't work with *these* kids." Or, just as bad: "I'm all about student voice and authentic engagement—but Manny, if you don't sit down and be quiet I'm taking away your points."

For teachers who define themselves as progressive, or socially conscious, or "woke," it's easy to point to other educators and call them out on how they're falling short. What's harder is seeing or acknowledging our own frailties and shortcomings, the moments when our actions collide spectacularly with our beliefs.

Even before that day with Manny, I'd tried to be honest with myself, to own up to my failures in the classroom—especially when I thought I was somehow betraying my beliefs about teaching and learning. But when it happens now, it's not just my own voice I hear in my head. It's Manny's as well, excited and insistent, reminding me to stay true to who I claim to be.

CHAPTER TWELVE

The Class Takes a Knee

"Mr. Michie! Mr. Michie!" A group of four girls rushed up to me on the way back to our classroom. I had just picked them up from one of their "special" classes.

"Ms. Byrne got really mad at Kasandra," one said.

"At Kasandra?" I asked. "What happened?" I wasn't surprised that Ms. Byrne had gotten irritated with my students. She was a regular substitute who had little patience for even minor disruptions, and some of the kids in my homeroom liked to push her buttons. But Kasandra? She never caused problems.

"When the pledge came on, a bunch of us didn't stand up," Cherish began.

Suddenly I knew exactly where this was going.

Although saying the pledge of allegiance each morning had gone out of favor long ago in many districts across the country, in Chicago some schools clung tightly to tradition. At Quincy, saying the pledge had been a ritual since—well, nobody really knew, but probably almost since the words were put to paper. The pledge was written in 1892—a time of rising nativism in the United States—and debuted the next year in Chicago schools during the World's Columbian Exposition.[1] Quincy opened its doors to a mix of Lithuanian, Polish, and Slav immigrant children just 3 years later.

Cherish went on: "So Ms. Byrne got mad and said, 'You need to stand. Get up.' But we stayed sitting."

"And then she started talking right to Kasandra," Zareen continued. "She said, 'Why aren't you standing up? What's wrong with you?'"

"And then," Cherish added, "she said, 'How dare you come to this country and get free schooling and free lunch when you won't even show respect for the flag?'"

"Whoa," I said. At least I think that's what came out of my mouth. Maybe I just thought it. "And what did Kasandra do?" I asked.

The girls' eyes all shifted to Cherish. She looked like she was about to burst out laughing. "She said, 'Ms. Byrne . . . have you even read the Constitution?'"

* * *

When Colin Kaepernick began the 2016 NFL preseason by choosing not to stand as the national anthem was played before a game, and fans reacted by posting online videos of his jersey being set aflame, I looked on not only as a sports fan and engaged citizen but as a teacher. And when I heard Kaepernick defend his actions, I knew the blowback from White America would be intense.

"I am not going to stand up to show pride in a flag for a country that oppresses Black people and people of color," Kaepernick said. "To me, this is bigger than football and it would be selfish on my part to look the other way."[2] If he couldn't, I thought, neither should we. I began the year in 8th-grade social studies with a short unit on the meaning of patriotism.

To kick things off, I asked small groups of students to discuss what the word *patriotism* meant and then share a short definition or example with the whole class. I jotted down their responses on the board:

- Being loyal to and respecting your country
- Agreeing to what your country is doing
- Supporting your country and showing favoritism toward it
- Celebrating your country like on the 4th of July
- To have pride and belief in your country
- Standing up for your country

Their ideas hewed closely to traditional definitions of the word. So, I posed a question for them to consider before we watched a few news reports on Kaepernick's anthem protest: "Is it 'unpatriotic' to speak out or protest against your country's government?"

As the unit continued over the next couple weeks, all my students stood for the pledge each morning. Not out of respect, necessarily, but out of habit. The practice had been drilled into them from the first day of preschool, and by 8th grade it seemed like the natural order of things, like grabbing a lunch tray or sharpening a worn-down pencil. I didn't like it for several reasons: It felt compulsory, even if it technically wasn't; many students didn't have a solid understanding of the pledge's meaning; and the words "with liberty and justice for all" didn't ring true for many of the young people I taught. But despite all this, I didn't discourage students from standing for the pledge or saying it.

Even as we moved deeper into the unit—analyzing quotes related to patriotism by Mark Twain and Emma Goldman and James Baldwin; learning about John Carlos and Tommie Smith's Black Power salute at the 1968 Olympics—I hadn't planned to make a connection to the pledge. I was thinking broader, and I missed that obvious connection. But somewhere along the line, students began to connect the dots on their own, and one day Nova articulated what a number of them had probably been thinking: "Isn't football players having to stand for the anthem kinda like us having to say the pledge? What if we don't believe the country is living up to it?"

I paused, but only for a moment. "You don't have to say it then."

"We don't?" Isaac asked. "Do we have to stand?"

"You don't have to. It's not a law."

"But we've always had to say it," Javier added. "Since we were little."

"It's an expectation at Quincy," I said. "At some other schools, too. But not everywhere. Nobody can make you stand up or say it."

That wasn't just my opinion. It was the Supreme Court's, in a 1943 decision that ruled schools could not force students to say or stand for the pledge. The majority opinion said, in effect, that just as the Bill of Rights protects a person's right to free speech, it also protects her right *not* to say something she doesn't wish to say.[3]

In the moment, the response from students was mostly muted. A number of kids seemed taken aback by the idea that they could have a choice in the matter. "Wait, *we* can protest?" they seemed to be thinking. It was a reminder of one of the ironies of teaching about popular resistance: It can be easier, for both teacher and students, to admire the idea of it from historical or geographical distance than to imagine actually setting something off in your own school.

Perhaps because of this, room 305's resistance to the pledge didn't begin with a storm of the barricades. It started gradually and quietly the next morning, with Nova and a couple other students staying seated while the rest of the class stood and delivered. By the end of the week, a few more had joined. A week or so after that, it was nearly half the class. The rest continued to stand as they always had, some speaking or mumbling the words, some silent.

As more kids joined the ranks of the protesters, though, the level of extraneous chatter during the pledge increased. I'd told the resisters from the beginning that I supported them and would defend their right to refuse participation. But I also insisted that they respect students who still wanted to say the pledge. That worked out fine at first, but as days went by, audible conversations often spilled over into the pledge's time. I tried quelling them with gentle reminders, but two days later the same thing would happen. One morning when a couple kids broke out in full-throated laughter in the middle of the recitation, I lost my patience.

"Look, I told you I support what you're doing, and I do. I'm proud of you for taking a stand. Or a seat. I respect your right to do it. But you also need to respect the rights of others who want to say the pledge by not disrupting them."

Even as the words came out of my mouth, I realized that protests in the world outside our classroom didn't, and shouldn't, always work that way. Sometimes infringing on the rights of the privileged and the powerful—shutting down an expressway or chanting in the middle of a trendy restaurant—seems to be the only way to get their attention. But these were 13-year-olds, and I was their teacher. I had to do my best to keep all their needs in mind.

* * *

My own earliest memories of the American flag were from my junior high years in the late 1970s. We didn't say the pledge in my elementary school—or if we did I have no memory of it—and I'd been too young to remember the flag's role in Vietnam-era protests. My father was a veteran of the Korean War, but neither he nor my mother were flag-waving types. I do recall the annual Fourth of July celebrations in Hickory Grove, the neighborhood where I spent those years: a parade, a teen beauty pageant, fireworks, and everything but the Porta-Johns draped in red, white, and blue.

I don't remember thinking much about what patriotism meant or feeling either love or disdain for my country. If anyone had asked 12-year-old me, I probably would have said the United States seemed like a great place, and why wouldn't it? I was White, and my family had enough resources to provide for my siblings and me. Still, I didn't feel a swell of pride when I saw the flag. I was mostly ambivalent toward it.

From an early age, though, I started to become aware of anti-Black racism. When I was four or five, my mother heard me utter the n-word. I must have overheard another kid say it, and I repeated it, as children do with new words, without knowing what it meant. But my mom didn't let it pass. She knelt down to my level, held me, and looked me in the eyes: "That is a hateful word," she said. "An awful, hateful word. I don't ever want to hear you say that word again." I don't have many vivid memories from that time of my life, but I never forgot that moment. I didn't fully understand her reaction, but I could see she was shaken, and that shook me. From that moment on, in my mind, that word was poison.

A couple years later, as a 1st grader, I was frightened by racist graffiti spray-painted on the home of a Black family who had recently moved in down the block from us. In school I heard White kids talk derisively about the Black community where my mother worked and my family attended church. One summer when I was about 10, in our church's small parking lot, I looked on as my mom pulled a business card from under our windshield wiper that read, "The Ku Klux Klan is watching you." White people who waved U.S. flags most proudly, I began to notice, were often also simmering with racial hatred. It wasn't uncommon in those days to see the American flag and the Confederate flag displayed side by side, an intermingling that was intentional and whose message, I later realized, was clear: American supremacy and White supremacy were close kin.

By the time I started teaching in 1990, the flag, for me, had come to signify nationalism, not patriotism or liberty or justice. It symbolized love of country only in the narrowest sense: an America-first, "We're number one" braggadocio backed with an even nastier flip side of xenophobia and racial hatred. So, I was intrigued when, at one of the first Chicago schools where I subbed, each day began not with the pledge but with a spoken affirmation of Black cultural identity. Instead of the national anthem, James Weldon Johnson's "Lift Ev'ry Voice and Sing" resounded through the loudspeakers.

When I came to Quincy the next year and saw how entrenched the pledge was, I was immediately uncomfortable with it. But since I didn't have a homeroom in those days, I didn't have to oversee the daily recitation. It was easy to ignore the issue, and for a while, I did. But one day, in my own moment of surreptitious insurrection, I climbed on top of a desk, took down my room's flag, rolled it up, and hid it in the back of a closet. Kids rarely noticed, but when someone did, we had great conversations about flags and symbols and nationalism and whether schoolchildren should be inducted into saying the pledge in schools in the first place.

A decade later when I returned to Quincy, the flag, not surprisingly, was back on display. I thought briefly about removing it again, but I decided against it. I'd learned long ago that you have to choose your battles as a teacher, and with all the other things I knew I'd have to deal with my first year back, I decided the fate of the flag wasn't something I wanted to spend my energy fighting.

* * *

As my students' pledge protest continued, one important consideration completely slipped my mind: Occasionally, the morning announcements would begin late, after class rotations had started, which meant the pledge would be recited when my students were in another teacher's class, not mine. If I had thought of this, I might have given the other teachers a heads-up. But I didn't. So, when half the class refused to stand in Ms. Byrne's class that day, she had been blindsided. That doesn't justify her response, but it was an important reminder to me that healthy communication among adults in a school matters, and if I'd let the other teachers know, the confrontation between Ms. Byrne and my students might have been avoided.

But she wasn't the only teacher who had been surprised by seeing students protest the pledge. Some kids in Nancy Ibarra's classes also weren't doing it, but when they stayed seated in their computer class, the teacher, Mr. Lituma, didn't berate them. Instead, he came to Nancy later that day to ask about it, she explained their reasoning, and he understood. Again, communication.

When I told Kim Goldbaum about what had happened with Ms. Byrne, she suggested I bring up the matter at our next PPLC meeting. The PPLC—Professional Personnel Leadership Committee—is an important but awkwardly named group of teachers at each school, mandated by state law in Illinois and charged with leading discussions on curriculum and instruction.[4] I wasn't that optimistic about how the conversation would go, but I agreed that bringing the issue of the pledge to the PPLC was a good idea.

When the meeting day arrived, I apologized for the lack of communication about my students' protest and the confusion it caused and reminded those in attendance that many schools in Chicago, maybe even most, no longer recited the pledge each day. Then, in a moment of runaway hopefulness, I decided to suggest that we survey all our school's teachers, and perhaps the students as well, about whether we should continue saying the pledge at all.

But traditions die hard, and traditions centered around professed devotion to country even harder. Most of the other teachers in the meeting had no interest in even taking a survey to see where people stood on the issue. They were content with the daily recitation. The pledge would live on at Quincy. On a positive note—at least from my perspective—our principal did affirm that students had the right to refuse to participate if they wished. Of course, Kasandra already knew that.

* * *

Two years later, with a different classroom of kids, I began the year with a new idea. I often say that I come up with only one truly original good idea each year as a teacher—everything else is adapted, borrowed, or straight-up swiped. I'm pretty sure this one was original, but maybe I'd read about a similar lesson somewhere. Either way, I was enthused about it.

Normally, when students come into class on the first day, my room is already decorated. I have lots of posters, provocative quotes, a few hand-lettered signs, some artifacts, and artwork. I usually leave just one bulletin board empty, and we quickly fill it up with family photos (an idea I stole), "Where I'm From" poems (swiped), or some other visual project that puts the kids' experiences front and center (almost always adapted or borrowed).

But I'd read Carla Shalaby's *Troublemakers*[5] over the previous summer, and it got me thinking anew about freedom in schools—freedom for kids to think for themselves, to make decisions about their classroom environment, to speak out, to *be*. In the past, I'd carefully chosen what I put on the walls of my classroom because I wanted my students to see what I valued, the kind of space I was hoping to create. But I realized that doing this, in some ways, made the classroom more mine than theirs.

So, instead of coming into a place that felt lived in, they'd entered on the first day to bare walls—I'd stripped our classroom of everything but the paint. I told them they were going to decide what went up and what didn't. A few days later, I laid all the posters and artwork and photos on desks around the classroom. I gave students 10 minutes to do a "gallery walk" and told them to think about a piece they wanted to keep on display.

"If you see something that you think has an important message or meaning, something that should be on our walls, you're going to have a chance to convince the rest of us," I told them. "If anyone else has a different opinion, they can voice that, too. And then you'll vote. Or, if there's anything you think shouldn't be on the walls, same thing: You have to make the case for why you think so."

After they'd made the rounds to view everything, I asked who wanted to go first. Angelica raised her hand. She got up from her desk and walked straight to the American flag which, like everything else, I'd removed from display. I was surprised but tried not to show it. I hadn't realized she was so passionate about having the flag.

Angelica glanced down at the red, white, and blue cloth hanging from her hands. She shifted her gaze to her classmates. Then she surprised me again. "I don't think we should have this flag in our room," she said. "It's supposed to represent freedom and equality, but based on what we've learned about past history and what's still happening now, I don't think it does. It doesn't seem like things are improving, either." Most of her classmates erupted in applause, though a few didn't join in.

I was a little thrown off by the turn of events. I hadn't seen it coming. I'd pitched the activity as an opportunity for them to decide what they wanted to have on display in our shared space, and had only thrown in the option of defending something that should be removed as an afterthought. Besides, unlike my homeroom from two years before, this group hadn't shown a strong opposition to the flag or the pledge. A few didn't stand, but it was never a movement that had gained momentum.

It was a reminder, though, that there is often far more going on in my students' minds than I know. And taken within the larger context of their lives, it shouldn't have been surprising at all. They had seen ICE agents on the streets of their neighborhood. They'd heard the president slander Mexicans as murderers and rapists, listened to all his talk about building a "beautiful" wall. They'd looked on as armored trucks and police vans occupied their blocks after a federal agent was shot in the community. From where they stood, freedom, equality, and justice were often in short supply.

By the end of the period, students had agreed on a number of items that should remain on our classroom's walls. Among them were two ceramic suns handmade in Mexico; a cartoon depicting the Statue of Liberty embracing a Muslim woman; an "undocumented and unafraid" poster; a replica of the Vietnam-era placard proclaiming "War is not healthy for children and other living things"; and a Black Lives Matter T-shirt.

The flag, along with the rest of the pieces that didn't elicit a defense, went back in the closet, locked up and out of sight. So far, no adult has noticed.

CHAPTER THIRTEEN

On the Side of the Child

I was sitting in a circle of chairs, surrounded mostly by young men I had known since they were my students as 7th and 8th graders. By this point, most were between 17 and 19 years old. They met every Wednesday night with a few adult mentors in a group known as Reflections. For an hour and a half each week, they talked about their lives, learned from guest speakers, and discussed readings that spoke to their experiences. I'd been helping out as a mentor, off and on, for nearly 20 years.

"What are some of the obstacles in your life right now?" I asked after we'd gone around the circle to check in. "What gets in your way?" I knew that many of the guys were struggling. Carlos had graduated from high school after being kicked out for a semester but now found himself stuck. Bryan dropped out toward the end of his sophomore year and spent several months in a youth detention center. Soon after being released, he became a father. Juan decided to leave high school 5 months short of graduation and enrolled in an alternative school.

"One thing during high school was a lack of support," said Carlos. "I feel like they kinda pushed troubled kids to the side, looked for ways to get rid of them rather than trying to support them."

Bryan agreed. "They don't let you give them feedback sometimes. They don't ask you, 'What do you think? How can we help you?'"

"Hell, yeah," Juan said. "I asked for engineering. But they didn't give it to me. I felt like they thought I couldn't succeed in that."

But navigating their educational futures was far from the only challenge these young men faced. And the hardships they confronted outside the classroom were not situated on parallel lines, separate and apart from their difficulties at school. They intersected.

"Even making it to school," Bryan said. "Just getting there without being harmed or nothing." During his freshman year, while on his way to school, he was chased for several blocks by a van full of guys from another neighborhood. "I was running like hell," Bryan remembered. "And I was like, 'What the fuck? I'm just trying to go to school, man.' And then you're in school trying to work on your project and trying to get your grades up and you're like, 'Fuck. Are they waiting for me outside?'" He shook his head. "That messes you up. It's hard to focus."

"And it's not just the other gangs—the police, too," Armando chimed in. "They be fuckin' with you. It's corrupt out here."

Money—or the lack of it—was also a worry that shadowed all the guys. "Not having enough to pay school fees," Bryan said, "or to have enough food in the crib."

"Yeah," added Carlos. "Sometimes when you don't eat, your body and mind ain't even gonna work right when you're trying to learn."

Many of the young men had mothers who worked hard at low-paying jobs to support them. But even that could be both blessing and curse. "They work long hours," Carlos said. "They wake up early, go to work, get home tired. They can't even help with the homework because most of our parents didn't get the education themselves. They're just trying to push through."

Carlos had hoped to be in college by this point, but his undocumented status made that—or finding steady work—difficult. He took day jobs on a construction crew when they needed extra help, but it was inconsistent. "I get in these bad moods with myself," he told me. "I feel useless. All this anger just builds up and I don't know what to do with it. And now that I can't get DACA [Deferred Action for Childhood Arrivals], what am I supposed to do?"

It was not a rhetorical question.

* * *

Teachers spend a lot of time thinking about what we want from our students. Many educators have specific expectations around students' work habits and effort and behavior and social skills. But what do we want *for* them—not just in the 10 months they are with us but in the years that follow?

I want the kids I teach to feel safe and free—in our school, in their community, and beyond. I want them to live in a city and country where they and their families and their cultural histories are embraced and valued, not maligned or targeted. I want them to see a justice system that works for all people, no matter their color or origin or circumstance. I want them to have access to the array of resources and opportunities that children in Chicago's wealthier neighborhoods have. I want them to have an equal shot at pursuing their dreams and an equal chance to live them out fully.

I'm guessing many teachers would nod along to at least some of the items on that list. In broad terms, we want good things for our students. But it seems there's often a disconnect somewhere, a failure to recognize that schools are not in an orbit of their own. What happens in the world outside the classroom is inextricably connected to what goes on inside it. Students walk out of our classrooms into lives that are shaped, and often constrained, by the social, cultural, political, and economic contexts in which they are situated.

Take these three examples:

Scene One: After school one day, a group of my Quincy colleagues is huddled in the second-floor hallway. I can tell from their body language that something is going on. I stop to listen in. I learn that one of their students, a 5th grader, went home from school the previous day to find that his father was gone. Taken by ICE. Soon to be deported. He and his younger sister are devastated.

Scene Two: I run into Sulema, a former student, working at a retail store near our school. I had last talked with her a year earlier, when she came by Quincy to let us know she would be heading to college in the fall. I ask how school is going. She winces. "Oh, I had to take a little break. I couldn't afford second semester tuition, and my parents can't really help much." She pauses. "But I'm planning to go back next year. I just gotta save some money."

Scene Three: I am walking to my car on a chilly evening, key in hand, trailed by two of my 8th-grade boys. Out of nowhere I hear the whoop of a siren and see beams of blue light bouncing off the pavement in front of me. In the time it takes me to realize what is happening, the teens I've just finished playing basketball with are up against the side of a police van, arms spread in front of them and legs splayed.

I try to plead with the two officers, both of whom appear to be White. I tell them, several times, that I am the boys' teacher, that they've been with me, that we just left a weekly Reflections group. I'm hoping, in the moment, that my whiteness or my adultness can be used as collateral, but the cops ignore me and continue the pat down. Finding nothing, they climb back into their van and rumble off.

"That's so messed up," I tell the guys once we are safely in my car.

"It happens all the time, Mr. Michie," one says. "That's our life."

It is not bad fortune that has befallen the young people in these three situations. It is bad policies. It is segregation and isolation and racism. It is an economic system that gives advantage to those whose pockets have been stuffed with advantages since birth. It is a city with a history of not showing equal concern for all its residents. A father is separated from his children partly because most of White America—including nearly 30% of teachers[1]—elected a president who branded Mexican immigrants as "murderers" and "rapists" and bragged about cracking down on "illegals." A girl drops out of school because her parents' hard work is compensated with low wages that allow only subsistence living. Eighth-grade boys are stopped by police because many Chicagoans are okay with it. They have convinced themselves that more aggressive policing equates to a safer, more "livable" city. Perhaps if their children were the ones being shoved against a van and frisked for no reason, treated as potential criminals for just walking down the street, they would see things differently. As for me, I can still hear myself saying over and over to the officers, "I'm their teacher! I'm their teacher! I'm their teacher!"

It is not enough to look at the situations faced by these three young people—or the hundreds of thousands like them in schools across our country—and simply say it is sad. It is also not enough for a teacher to walk into a school in an impoverished community each day and say to himself, "I'm doing my part just by showing up. I'm a good person for being here." It is not enough simply to be in the same space with our students. We also have to be *with* them—in solidarity, in their corner, on their side.

To recognize this is to acknowledge that, as teachers, we cannot separate our classroom selves from our citizen selves. Teaching is political—not in the sense of candidates and parties and election-day hysteria, but in the sense that the personal is political, that our lives and our work are part of an expansive and interconnected social fabric. Inequity in the broader society impacts what happens in schools and vice versa. As teachers, we need to attend to both.

* * *

For some teachers, being "good" means knowing the prescribed curriculum, mastering instructional techniques, maintaining order, and producing high-scoring students. In the documentary *Fear and Learning at Hoover Elementary*[2] (still relevant, sadly, 20 years after its release), we meet Dianne, a White teacher in a school of mostly Mexican and Central American children in Los Angeles. Outside Hoover, the city is embroiled in controversy over a proposed state law that would deny public services to undocumented immigrants. Inside the school, Dianne has a reputation as one of its best teachers. She says she is "up on curriculum" and boasts that all her students "read at grade level or above." When she closes the classroom door, she says, she does "what's best for those kids" and is "there for them one hundred percent."[3]

But the film reveals a more complicated picture. Outside her classroom, Dianne has little patience for people who wave the Mexican flag while protesting the proposed law. "If they love Mexico and have that much pride, go back," she says. She believes the United States should crack down on undocumented immigrants: "The children who belong here need be taken care of and there's gonna be no money left . . . people need to know, you can't come here and break a law." And she is frustrated that her students are slow to embrace "American" norms: "Most of my kids are born in Los Angeles . . . how dare they live in this country and not learn English?. . . . I'm not saying don't keep your culture, but if you choose to come to America, you have to give up something."[4]

Dianne draws a sharp line between her teacher self and her citizen self. That the policies reflected in her rhetoric cause harm to the families of children she teaches every day—the ones she says she supports "one hundred percent"—doesn't seem to faze her. As she sees it, her responsibility to her students is bound by the specifics of her job description. It begins when she enters the classroom and ends when she walks out the door.

My Quincy colleague, Patty Wagner, sees it differently. "These are *our* kids," she tells me. "I look at them and I see my own children. And when they are in a situation and they're powerless to do anything about it, how can we not try to do something?"

One year, the day after Valentine's, Patty was setting up her projector when she overheard two 7th-grade boys talking about what had happened to them the afternoon before. They were walking to the park after school when a police car pulled up. Two officers got out, threw them up against a fence, and frisked them. Patty, who is White, says she was stunned to hear the story. It was totally unlike anything in her experience or the experience of her own children. "I was just thinking, 'This is illegal! They can't do that!'" The image she couldn't shake, she says, was what the officers found in one of the boys' pockets when they searched him: No weapons. No drugs. Just a rose his mom had given him for Valentine's.

A month or so later, when I told Patty about my experience witnessing a different pair of our students—both of whom were in her homeroom—being stopped and frisked by police without justification, she decided she had to speak up. She wrote a letter to the police district commander expressing her dismay at the officers' lack of regard for her students' rights in both cases. "I was very upset," she says. "I remember writing that what happened to these boys would never happen in my neighborhood, to my own children. So, it shouldn't happen to our students, either."

Patty doesn't use the term *political* to describe the actions she took on behalf of her students. She says she was advocating for them. But she clearly sees a connection between supporting kids inside the classroom and speaking up against the injustices they experience outside it.

In communities of color, the notion that teaching and learning are political has rarely been controversial. There is a deep historical understanding of the need to intertwine traditional views of education—the three Rs—with political conceptions of learning. Literacy was important to enslaved Africans because of its potential as an emancipatory tool. During the civil rights movement, "freedom schools" connected the education of Black youth to the larger struggle for racial equality and justice. Mexican students walked out of their schools in East Los Angeles in 1968 to demand they be taught their own cultural history by teachers who looked like them. Indigenous people fought for control of their own education with the creation of tribal colleges. In all these instances, learning was tied to self-empowerment and community uplift. It was always political.

Several of my colleagues at Quincy are heirs to this tradition. "I don't have confidence in politics," says Nancy Ibarra, who is Mexican American. "From when I was a kid until now, I've seen how politics has never helped my people. I've never felt like, 'Oh, this candidate is going to take us to where we need to be,' because over and over they've shown that they're not going to do that." As a teacher, Nancy says, she focuses on helping students think about their own agency rather than putting all their hopes in elected leaders. "I feel it's kind of fighting against [party] politics. Finding a way to go around it. What are we, regular citizens, going to do to survive what these politicians are doing to us—or not doing for us? As a teacher, I feel I have the responsibility to talk with kids about that."

Nancy takes this beyond the classroom as well. When she learned about Dreamers and Allies Run, a group of young adults in Back of the Yards who were running in the Chicago marathon as a way to raise money to fund scholarships for undocumented students, she signed up. She collected pledges as a runner for several years and now volunteers to help interview scholarship candidates. "For me, it's personal," Nancy says. "I've always been part of a mixed-status family. And seeing students hoping to go off to college and then having to face this wall where they can't go on, only because they're undocumented—it's so unfair. When kids leave this building, they have to deal with these policies, and if you're not addressing that as a teacher, you're not teaching the whole child. You're teaching a fraction of the child."

Saraí Jimenez, who is Mexican and grew up only a few blocks from Quincy, says almost any choice she makes in her 1st-grade classroom is political. "If you separate your kids in boys' and girls' lines—you're defining something there. What you choose to teach: if I teach about Cesar Chavez versus another person, or the books I choose to read to my students. That's all political. Some teachers try to say, 'Oh, no, no, no. Nothing political. I'm just here to teach.' But that statement itself is political."

Just as she keeps one eye on the messages her organizational and curricular choices communicate to her students, Saraí also keeps an eye on the larger contexts of her students' lives. When the increased presence of U.S. immigration officers in the community prompted her 6- and 7-year-olds to ask if their parents would be deported, she not only tried her best to reassure them, she took action. "When something like that happens and we have students in front of us, the question should be, 'What can we do? How can we support them?'"

Some of the undocumented parents of Saraí's students came to her for advice. Where could they go for assistance? Who was trustworthy? How much would they charge? She had worked with the immigration committee at her local parish since she was in college and decided that one way she could help parents—and Quincy teachers—was to provide informational workshops that would answer some of their most pressing questions. The sessions covered topics such as knowing your rights with the police and ICE, preparing an emergency plan for your children, and finding legal assistance. "I see it as an extension of my teaching," Saraí says. "If my students have an issue, it's my issue, too. It affects all of us."

For Kim Goldbaum, teaching is inseparable from her intersecting identities. "I'm a teacher. I'm Black. I'm a socialist. I'm a woman. I'm a unionist. And I bring all that into the classroom. We all do. We bring everything that we think, and everything that we are." In Kim's language arts and social studies classes, that means studying the word choice and repetition in Sojourner Truth's "Ain't I a Woman" speech.

It means not only analyzing the lyrics of civil rights songs like "Keep Your Eyes on the Prize" but singing them—with gusto—as a group. It means dissecting news articles about racial profiling. And sometimes it means being silly. "It's an extension of my personality," she says. "I'm goofy. I see humor in a lot of things. Kids need to think, but they need to laugh, too."

Even after long days of teaching and staying after school to assess student work or attend meetings, Kim usually doesn't head straight home. "I do a lot of rallying for things that I believe in," she says. "Marches against school closings and the lack of funding, but also anti-police brutality, women's marches, #MeToo, reproductive justice. And the reason I add my body to these spaces is that these issues affect me. They impact my neighborhood. So, I try to do what I can. But one person's voice is not that important until it's amplified with the voices of others. I believe in the power of collectivity."

That, Kim points out, is also a political idea—one that clashes with the notion of rugged individualism that has long been promoted in American schools. But standing alone, while sometimes necessary, can be bruising to the soul, especially for adolescents on the cusp of self-discovery. Having peers and teachers on your side—not just in the abstract but truly on your side—can make all the difference.

* * *

Jonathan was a kid who could disappear in the classroom if you let him. He was unassuming, mild-mannered, and almost never drew attention to himself. But a little more than midway through his 7th-grade year at Quincy, the attention came anyway. A few classmates started asking him: *Is it true? Do you like guys?* The questions took him by surprise. He'd only confided in one friend—not even his parents or siblings knew at that point—and he'd trusted her not to share with anyone.

At first, he denied it or brushed aside the questions. He was afraid of how his classmates might react. He thought they might see or treat him differently. But he decided to tell a couple girls in his homeroom—his closest friends. When they responded supportively, he came out to his teacher, Nancy, and then to the rest of his class. "It was an emotional thing," he remembers. "They made posters for me. People hugged me. Ms. Ibarra was crying. My friends were crying. Everybody was so supportive. And I was so relieved."

Nancy asked Jonathan if he thought it would be a good idea to go around and speak to each 7th- and 8th-grade class. He said he thought it would help stop the rumors and questions, and he wanted other students to hear it directly from him. He was ready to speak his truth, to let everyone know.

At that point, Nancy could have hesitated. She could have worried about seeking approval from the principal or the Board of Education. But she didn't. She understood that Jonathan had been hurting and that he needed her help in that moment. She made a decision, right then and there, to do what he needed her to do. During the kids' recess, she gave the rest of us on the upper-grade team a heads-up about his plan.

I was hopeful but also a little uneasy about how my students' might respond. I had done my best to use gender inclusive language and to normalize discussions of sexual and gender identities in my classroom, and overall students had been open and respectful. Some, of course, had family members who were gay or lesbian. But I still had to address homophobic comments or slurs on occasion—mostly from boys—and I knew that teasing and harassment often happened out of earshot of a teacher. I didn't want Jonathan to have to deal with any of that.

After lunch, Jonathan walked into my class, went to the front of the room, and said, "I have something to say. I know a lot of you may have been hearing things about me." He paused. The silence was complete. "So, I just wanted to come here and let you all know: I am gay." He paused again. Students applauded. Jonathan exhaled and smiled. I looked around the room, tears filling my eyes. It was a beautiful moment, and beautiful moments followed in every classroom Jonathan came out to that day. In Lorel Madden's 8th-grade homeroom, the students called him back after he'd left for an extended group hug. Even 4 years later, when I talked with him about it, he still had only positive memories of that day and the weeks and months afterward.

It would be hard to backtrack and identify the precise factors that led to Jonathan feeling so embraced by his peers. But it wasn't simply luck or coincidence. GLSEN's Annual School Climate Survey found in 2017[5] that LGBTQ middle-school students "reported a more hostile school climate" than high schoolers, as well as more discrimination, more frequent anti-LGBTQ remarks, and less access to LBGTQ resources and supports. I wouldn't say we were a consciously safe school for LGBTQ kids, but as an upper-grade team, we definitely did some things right. We called out homophobic name-calling and bullying and tried to educate kids who engaged in it. Our classroom libraries featured books with LGBTQ protagonists and themes. Several of our classes had viewed and discussed Teaching Tolerance's documentary film about antigay harassment, *Bullied*. My students had written essays the previous year about what a school that supports and validates LGBTQ youth should look like. It wasn't always a comprehensive or concerted effort, but we had laid a foundation.

When I talked with Jonathan about his coming-out experience, he told me his freshman year of high school had been filled with a barrage of verbal and physical harassment. Despite "safe space" posters in the hallways, few people—kids or adults—intervened. Eventually, he ended up transferring to an alternative school where, thanks to a gay–straight alliance group and supportive adults and peers, he again felt fully embraced.

Thinking back on his time at Quincy, Jonathan said the environment of inclusion in our classrooms had been an important factor in why he'd felt so affirmed. "I think it was mostly because of the atmosphere," he said. "All the teachers supported me and that made me feel safer. We were all taught not to be prejudiced, and to treat everyone how you would want to be treated."

In a time where brazen public displays of hatred are on the rise, that may sound like an old-fashioned, even quaint idea. But when taken seriously in schools, it is a political one as well.

CHAPTER FOURTEEN

Uncertain Certainty

I beat myself up the entire drive home. Played everything back in my head. Cursed at myself for such miserable teaching. *You knew the documentary could upset kids. How could you not be more prepared for their reaction? How could so many students leave the room feeling beaten down? And in tears? What is your fucking problem?*

The documentary in question was *Latinos Beyond Reel,*[1] a 2013 film about the representation of Latinx in mainstream U.S. media. It traces the history of Latinx stereotyping in Hollywood movies, TV shows, and cartoons, and examines the real-world impact of such depictions. The final section shows clips of YouTube videos posted by White kids, who appear to be between 12 and 16 years old, in which they role-play as border agents "killing beaners" with realistic-looking automatic weapons. Another clip shows a video game where the objective is to shoot as many Mexican "drug smugglers" or "breeders"—women carrying children across the U.S. border—as possible. It's a devastating sequence that lingers long after the final shot has faded.

I knew all this going in, of course. I'd used the film before with my 7th and 8th graders, and it had sometimes left students shaken. Still, I thought the documentary was important to see and discuss, especially since some students shrug off stereotypes—even those that degrade their own racial or cultural group—as essentially harmless attempts at humor. "It's just a meme, Mr. Michie," is a justification I've heard numerous times. But *Latinos Beyond Reel* makes a strong counterargument that the destructive power of such misrepresentations shouldn't be dismissed.

Having learned from past viewings, I thought I had laid the groundwork to prepare students for the potential emotional impact of the film and to minimize the distress it might cause. Before we began viewing it, I delivered my own version of a viewer discretion advisory: "Just so you know—some parts of this documentary are intense. It might bring up some strong emotions for some of you. It might make you upset."

"We're gonna cry?" a student asked, jokingly.

"Some people might," I said, not breaking a smile. "Students have before. And however you react, the main thing is we need to support each other. It may not hit you as hard as it does the person sitting next to you. But everybody is entitled to their own emotional response. So, no making fun of anybody. Honor every person's feelings." What I hadn't taken into account fully, I later realized, was just how much heavier the film might land on my students in the age of Trump.

I stopped the documentary at numerous points along the way so we could discuss its main themes: how Hollywood films recast history to portray Whites as perpetual heroes and Mexicans as villains; how a Spanish accent or darker skin can limit roles offered to Latinas; how Latinx activists continue to push for more dignified and accurate representations of their communities. Students were into it, and the inclusion of a few throwback media clips they recognized kept their attention. When the title card for the film's final section flashed on screen, I paused the video and repeated an abridged version of my message from the day before: *This last section is intense. It may upset you. Whatever emotions you have, it's okay. We'll talk about it.*

But we didn't talk about it. When I stopped the video, the room still dark except for a bluish glow from the screen, the class was almost silent. I heard only muffled sobbing. Mireya put her head down on her desk, her shoulders shaking. Antonio just stared straight ahead, jaw clenched, a mix of anger and hurt in his eyes.

I let the silence envelop the room for a bit. I asked students to raise their hands if they felt angry or hurt, and nearly the whole class did. I posed a few questions. But nobody was in the mood to share. Fernando, who was usually ready with a joke no matter the occasion, shook his head, his eyes red with tears. He looked completely crushed. The whole room did. And it was my lesson that had crushed them.

* * *

Back in my younger days as a teacher, I was occasionally told by colleagues that I needed to focus on more upbeat themes in my classroom. One told me the topics students tackled in my media classes were too intense. Another made a comment along similar lines: "These kids have enough hard things in their lives already. School should be a place where they feel happy. We should be lifting them up, not bringing them down."

I remember that last part stinging. I'd never thought I was bringing my students down. It definitely wasn't my intent. But I could understand where my colleagues were coming from. Teaching with an eye on broader issues of injustice often means having kids take hard looks at complex, seemingly intractable problems. It can be discouraging. Dispiriting. Overwhelming. It's a lot to put on the backs of 12- and 13-year-olds, and I tried to keep that in mind when I planned units and projects. No matter the topic, I sought to highlight ways people had come together in moments of resistance, compassion, or hope.

At the same time, I also tried to make space for kids to be kids. Although I believed my students genuinely appreciated being seen as informed, thoughtful people who cared about the world around them, they also liked to laugh, goof around, and have fun. So, in addition to creating media projects that examined homophobia or the plight of undocumented students, we also did silly parodies of navel-gazing reality shows and Spanish-language novelas. In one novela scene a group of 7th graders created, a girl angrily confronts a classmate about the whereabouts of a friend. The dramatic conversation builds until the friend shows up: She's been in the bathroom the whole time. For many middle school kids, this is comedy gold.

The question, for me, is not whether adolescents are willing or able to confront difficult issues that impact their own families and communities. From what I've seen and experienced, they clearly are. The question, then, is how to do so without leaving them feeling disempowered in the process. One of the central paradoxes of being a teen is that just as you begin growing into your own power more fully, you are simultaneously becoming more aware of injustices you seem to have no control over. You are at once testing the limits of your budding power while feeling draped by a cloak of powerlessness.

For teens of color, poor kids, LGBTQ students, and other marginalized young people, this polarity can be even more pronounced. The cloak is thicker and the struggle to wrestle it off more daunting. For some, it may not even seem worth the effort. After all, what if you spend all your energy fighting to throw it off, and you still find yourself shouting into a void? What if it doesn't matter? What if nothing changes? What if nobody cares?

That's exactly the argument one of my 8th graders, Ruby, had made to her classmates the year before. When her friend, Analise, suggested that the class create a Twitter hashtag to promote positive media representations of Latinxs, Ruby quickly shot the idea down. "Nobody cares what we say," she said. "Nobody's gonna listen to us."

"How do you know?" Analise replied. "We could at least try. Maybe people will listen. You never know."

"Yeah, you could go ahead and create the hashtag," Ruby said. "But it's not like it's gonna go viral. It's not gonna change anything."

Other students in the class were divided on whether they could make an impact. But many seemed to agree with Ruby: *Nobody's gonna listen to us. It's not gonna change anything.* Analise said she would try to come up with a hashtag for the class to use, but a few days later spring break arrived, and by the time we returned to class the following week, the idea and its momentum had fizzled. But just as quickly, another one took its place.

* * *

I began to see daily tweets from Mariame Kaba (@prisonculture), an activist and educator based in New York, about donating money to create a monument in Chicago dedicated to the life and work of journalist and antilynching crusader Ida B. Wells. Wells's descendants had been trying to get the monument built for years, but their fundraising efforts had stalled. Kaba had taken up the cause to help raise the needed dollars. "I'd like to point out," she tweeted, "that there isn't a single monument dedicated to ANY woman in Chicago. NOT. A. ONE. . . . We can change this by building a monument uplifting Ida's legacy, work, and life."

Ida B. Wells's antilynching work had been part of my social studies curriculum for several years. Students read one of her speeches, "This Awful Slaughter," learned about death threats she'd faced for speaking out against the lynching of Black Americans, and discussed how she used the media to bring these horrors to the consciousness of White people. "The way to right wrongs is to turn the light of truth upon them,"[2] Wells wrote, and for many of my students, this struck a chord. They were inspired by Wells's tireless efforts to ensure that Black lives mattered, and I thought some would want to contribute to the monument fund, even if it was just a small amount.

I presented the idea to my classes the next day. By day's end we'd collected $10.75—seven dollars of that from one 7th grader who emptied out his pocket and gave everything he had. A few days later, we were up to $26.75, and I told my students I would match whatever they donated. If they could bring their contributions up to $50, I said, my $50 would make our total donation $100. That might not seem like an ambitious goal, but I knew that many families in Back of the Yards were living check to check, struggling to pay bills and keep their children clothed and fed. In contrast, schools on Chicago's north side routinely raised thousands of dollars, even tens of thousands, from parent donations. Then again, that money often went to things like lab equipment or sports uniforms, not to publicly honor a Black woman who dedicated her life to antiracist work.

As days went by, the donations added up—often coin by coin. A 7th grader fished 75 cents out of his pocket after lunch one day to add to the total. A parent came by after school with her daughter and handed me an envelope with "$10 for Ida B. Wells" written on the front. "Maya told me what you guys are doing," the mom said, "and we wanted to help out." Altogether, the students were now up to $103.30.

I posted an update on Twitter about how much the kids had raised, adding that I planned to match their total. Erin McGurk, a school district administrator in Connecticut, was inspired by their work and responded that she, too, would match whatever they raised. Mariame Kaba also commented on their efforts in a series of tweets:

> A few words about these moving and kind gestures being made by middle-school students in Chicago. . . . Children/youth understand some things about fairness and kindness that we lose as we get older. Anyone who's been around children for any time at all will at some point hear the "but that's not fair" refrain. They really, really care about things being *fair*. Somehow as we get older, we seem to lose that instinct. So it makes sense to me that middle school students would be drawn to Ida B. Wells and to her strong sense of fairness and her relentless pursuit of justice. It makes sense to me that they would get behind an effort to honor her legacy. I'm beyond moved by their contributions to this effort. I'm so grateful that they are offering what they can. They are such a model for the rest of us.[3]

The next day, I showed students the matching pledge and read them Mariame's comments on their work. This seemed to give them added motivation. They could see evidence that their efforts were being noticed. A quarter here and a dollar there, the donations kept coming. On the last day of the 2-week fundraiser, Adan, an 8th grader, pulled two tightly rolled bills from his pocket and handed them to me. I unfurled them. It was two twenties.

"Adan—that's too much," I said without even thinking. I didn't know much about his home situation, but I knew forty dollars was a lot for many families.

"I want to," he said. "It's not my parents' money. It's mine. I want to donate it."

"Are you sure?"

"I'm sure," he said. "All of it."

A common knock on teens is that it's all about them—what they want, what they need. But I was often blown away by my students' generosity of spirit.

Adan's $40 brought the final total to $211.28, much of it from small donations of a couple dollars or less. Combined with my match and

Erin's, that made it $633.84. When I posted that on Twitter, Mariame replied that she, too, would match the students' donations, and challenged others to do the same. When all was said and done, the students were responsible for $1,106.40 in donations to the Ida B. Wells monument project.

When I projected that number on the screen the next day, trekking through 2 weeks of tweets to show how their initial $10.75 had multiplied again and again, kids looked at each other, wide-eyed. "Damn!" one said, more to himself than to anyone else. I could feel a kinetic charge in the room, an energy that came from the realization that what they were doing was making a difference.

Fundraising isn't the pinnacle of activism, of course. But in this instance, money was what was needed. And while my students' $1,110 total was a drop in the bucket of the $300,000 goal, it mattered. By that July, the project would be fully funded.[4] Our city would, in the not-too-distant future, have a public monument dedicated to a Black woman, a freedom fighter, Ida B. Wells. And when that day came, these students could visit and know that, in their own small way, they helped make it happen.

* * *

I tried to summon some inspiration from that experience as I thought about how to respond to what had happened with *Latinos Beyond Reel.* I didn't have many options. Winter break was just 2 days away, so embarking on a larger project was out of the question. We'd taken students out into the community to protest in the past—to participate in a "We Belong" rally after the 2016 election, for a pro-immigrant march in 2017, and as part of the #Enough movement for stronger gun laws in early 2018—but there was no time to organize anything like that. It was tempting just to leave it behind, to spend our last day before the break watching *Coco* or playing games. Something fun, something less intense, something to take their minds off the anger and sadness they'd felt.

But I couldn't just let it go. I had to address it. I wouldn't be able to bring a sense of healing or restoration in a 50-minute class period, but maybe I could at least provide a space to be heard, to say what needed to be said. Sometimes there's power in just doing that.

The next day, I began the class by asking students to respond in writing to a prompt:

> Do you think I should continue to show this documentary to future classes or not? Are the issues it brings up important to consider, even though it can be triggering? Or is it too upsetting to use in a classroom setting?

After spending some time writing, several students offered to share their thoughts. "I don't think you should show it because it brings up a lot of sadness—and it's triggering to watch," said Vero.

"Yeah, for kids who have immigrant parents, they might get scared that some of the things they show in the movie might happen to their parents," added Carlos. "I think for really sensitive people it's way too hard to see it."

Juliana, one of the students who had been most visibly affected by the film, had a different point of view. "For me it was upsetting," she said, "but I think showing it will help us think about how we can fix this issue. I cried a lot, and I'm still upset, but what I'm trying to figure out now is how to do something about this situation."

Noel agreed: "I think you should show it because when you see it and realize the history and all the negative ways Latinos have been shown, you can come back with more power and have more of a voice about it."

The pain was still fresh for many of the kids. But as they shared their reflections, I sensed that even though I was the one who'd provoked their hurt, my students understood that I hadn't intended to harm them. They trusted me. It was a trust built on a foundation of weeks and months of respectful interactions, and it was strong enough not to shatter over a single misstep. That may seem like a small thing, but if it's true that relationship building is at the heart of good teaching—and I believe it is—the importance of trust is hard to overstate.

After the students shared, I gave each of them a square of white paper and a Sharpie. I told them to use the paper to get out any leftover feelings or thoughts they wanted to express about the film. They could write just a single word or fill up the entire paper. If drawing helped, they could do that as well.

Unlike with some other writing assignments, when kids just sat and pondered or zoned out for a couple minutes before getting started, with this one, the words poured forth:

> Anger
> disappointment
> Fear
> HATRED
>
> I'm not an alien, I'm a human!!!
>
> Disappointed in this so-called humanity.
>
> How I felt after seeing the film was scared because it's scary to see how some teenagers want to "kill" Mexicans just because they're immigrants.
>
> outraged
> offended
> Infuriated
>
> heartbreaking
>
> I felt bad for the people that got triggered watching the documentary. I also felt disrespected that they misrepresented Mexicans and Latinos and are making us all look bad.
>
> I am angry about the film, but I understand why it was made.

When the students finished writing, we all went out into the hall together. I'd cleared off a bulletin board that morning, and they took turns stapling their papers to it. With each staple that punctured the surface, each note that went up, the tension seemed to lift a bit. Of course, we hadn't addressed the underlying issue. We hadn't even talked much about what that might look like, about what we could do, if anything, to engage, to take action, to speak out in a larger way. But it was a beginning: Acknowledging the hurt, naming its cause. The kids seemed to feel a little better, and I did, too. Was that enough, though? I wasn't sure. Would I show the film again next year? I wasn't sure about that, either.

It might seem that a teacher with nearly 3 decades of experience would have a more definitive notion of how to handle a situation like this one. Maybe there are some teachers out there who would. But one of the most obvious lessons I'd learned in my return to teaching had been this: Despite all my previous classroom experience, despite all the reading and theorizing I'd done in my doctoral program, despite a decade as a professor of education, I still, almost daily, wondered if I was doing the right thing with a particular kid or lesson or circumstance. I questioned myself, second-guessed decisions, as a matter of course.

In my worst moments, this struck me as a weakness. An experienced teacher should *know*, should be sure, should have the answers—like so many educational writers and professional development gurus seem to. But then I'd remember Paulo Freire, who, in his book *Teachers as Cultural Workers*,[5] writes that humility and "uncertain certainty" are essential qualities for progressive educators. For Freire, humility does not equate to deference or meekness. It signifies, instead, both self-respect and a respect for others. "Humility," he writes, "helps me avoid being entrenched in the circuit of my own truth. . . . No one knows it all; no one is ignorant of everything. We all know something; we are all ignorant of something."[6]

Teaching with uncertain certainty means that I can stand firm in my core beliefs while still being unsure at times of how best to enact them. It means that I can—that I must—listen to and learn from my students and their perspectives on the world. It means that, like the adolescents I teach, I am neither all-powerful nor completely powerless—in the classroom or outside it. It means acknowledging that uplift and positive change can sometimes be born out of painful awakenings. And it means that when I make a mistake, even a big one, I can find a way forward, even if I don't know for sure where it will lead.

CHAPTER FIFTEEN

Do Not Forget to Reach

I had returned to Quincy in 2012 committing, in my mind, only to a year. One hundred and eighty school days. I hoped it would be longer than that, but I wasn't sure if I was up to the task. I didn't know how I'd feel about being back, if I'd enjoy the challenge like I had the first time around. I didn't know if I'd still be able to build strong relationships with the kids, if I could do a good job without running myself ragged. I didn't know if I could do a good job, period.

Six and a half school years later, I'd say the results have been mixed. My annual teacher evaluations are hovering at an average score of about 324 out of 400. What does that mean? According to the Board of Education's arbitrary numerical formula, it means I'm a "proficient" teacher. What does that mean? That I'm a step better than "developing" but also a step short of "excellent." What does that mean? To me, not much. Depending on the day or the hour, I could fit into any of those three categories.

If I were to do my own teacher evaluation—not with the Charlotte Danielson framework, thank you—I'd be happy with some aspects of my work and disappointed with others. I think I've done a good job of continuing to develop original curriculum, and of planning units and projects that both challenge students and provide multiple ways for them to show what they've learned. I'm gratified to see how much the culture of independent reading has changed in my classroom, and how providing students with a choice of what to read, along with shelves full of great books by authors from diverse backgrounds, has translated into a greater love of reading for many kids. I like that I've made space for recurring connections between the school and the community outside, whether with student-produced videos or guest speakers or learning about the area's history or creating virtual tours of the neighborhood. I'm still attentive to student feedback and criticism, and I think I have a good handle on what's working well and what's not.

What's not? I could probably fill a few pages with areas in which I still need to grow as a teacher, as it's typically easier for me to see my weak spots than my strengths. But a few things stand out. One that's a nearly constant frustration is assessment. It's not that I don't know what quality assessment looks like or how to design it. I do. I even taught about it when I was a professor. The problem is finding time to give consistent, meaningful, substantive, timely feedback. With 150 students, I just can't do it. More often than not, I end up simply assigning grades rather than providing helpful comments or zeroing in on specific areas for improvement. Although most kids don't complain as long as they get a good score, that doesn't make it acceptable. I know I'm failing sometimes at helping kids understand exactly what they need to do better and how they can get there.

I fall short, too, when it comes to parent engagement. As a professor working with future teachers, I emphasized the importance of valuing, seeking input from, and listening to parents and caregivers. And at our school's semiannual parent–teacher conferences, I keep that advice in mind. I try to spend as much time listening as I do talking. I speak Spanish when it's needed. I let parents know that I appreciate them. But in between conferences—the other 30-something weeks of the school year—my interactions with caregivers are too infrequent. Sure, I call if I have a serious concern about a child. But I don't engage with them on a regular or consistent basis. I get buried in other demands, and connecting with parents gets unintentionally pushed to the side. My intentions are good. Every school year for the past 4 years, I've told myself I am going to create a monthly newsletter to update parents and other caregivers on our class activities. But I still haven't published a single issue.

I also continue to struggle with meeting the unique needs—learning and otherwise—of each student in my classes. Seeing the student is one thing; figuring out how to respond to what you're seeing, 30 kids at a time, 150 kids a day, is another. Leslie loves to read graphic novels but has a hard time comprehending nonfiction. Roberto just arrived from Mexico and understands almost no English. Elsa is sweet and amazingly adept at technology but has a severe learning disability and needs frequent one-on-one attention. Alicia is eager to participate but confided to me that she doesn't feel challenged in class. Sergio comes in, drops his book bag with a thud, and is usually asleep within the first 5 minutes. Ethan told me he thinks he has PTSD. And there are 23 others, each with a singular story and journey—and four other classes, also full of kids who bring their own urgent questions and quirky personalities and beautiful struggles. It's mind-blowing, really, that any teacher can meet all those needs, can respond with the kindness and resolve and patience and attentive listening it requires. I try. But, to riff on a phrase from Cornelius Minor,[1] I am not always as successful as they need me to be.

Teaching at 56 is not the same as it was at 27. I feel the years creeping up on me. I'm often flat-out exhausted by day's end, and I can't run the floor during the annual student–teacher basketball game like I used to. But I'm not burned out or dispirited or jaded. I try to stay fresh, to seek out new ideas and resources, to listen to and learn from the voices of a younger generation of teachers. Besides, despite the self-assurance that comes with years of experience, old insecurities still pop up. I am reminded, probably daily, that teaching is not something you figure out after 3 or 5 or even 20 years, and then just sit back and press repeat.

One of my mentors used to say, "When you think you have it all figured out—that's when you begin to die as a teacher."

I haven't started dying yet.

* * *

Quincy, too, is alive and kicking but not without a fight. In the fall of 2016, we were informed that our annex building—a former Catholic school across the street that houses all our 3rd- and 4th-grade classrooms—was slated to be closed. According to CPS's calculations, the space was "underutilized." Their plan was for us to move the 175 students from the annex—or "the branch," as we call it—to our main building.

How they expected that to happen without serious adverse consequences for students was hard to fathom. We had only one small unoccupied classroom—and even that was being utilized for an office that would then need to be shifted someplace else. To fit all our students in one building, class sizes throughout the grades would balloon, and we'd lose dedicated classrooms for art, library, technology, and students with special needs. One CPS administrator even posed the idea of converting our gymnasium stage to a classroom in order to maximize space. Could we? I suppose. But I sure wouldn't want to be the one trying to teach there.

When I first heard about the threatened closure, my mind wandered back to 2014, when Chicago's mayor, Rahm Emanuel, closed 50 CPS schools. I had similar thoughts to those I'd had then: This wouldn't happen to White kids. It wouldn't happen on the north side. Some White Chicagoans would surely scoff at such a suggestion. *Why does it always have to be about race?* they'd say. *It's about shifting populations, about the city's troubled finances.* But those factors, even if legitimate, are not separate from matters of race and racism. They're intertwined. Chicago remains one of the most segregated cities in the United States, and it got that way not by chance, but by design—through redlining and "contract sales" and restrictive covenants and strategically placed public housing.[2] Many decades later, the legacies of these practices remain. White neighborhoods get their streets cleaned, their potholes filled, and their snow shoveled on time. They don't get their schools closed.

Despite that, it was undeniable that our school's enrollment had been declining for several years. The reasons were easy enough to identify: families embracing the promises of newly opened charter schools, or moving elsewhere to seek safety from the violence in the neighborhood. Either way, the impact was visible. Class sizes in the upper grades were still mostly around 30, but in the primary grades, some classes had only 20 students. In many private and suburban elementary schools, of course, a 20-to-1 student-teacher ratio is the norm, or at least the goal: Smaller class sizes give teachers greater opportunity to work with students individually. But in CPS, where school closings have become a favored strategy for cutting costs and jump-starting so-called reform efforts, it's an opportunity.

When word of the proposed closure of Quincy's branch got out, parents, community members, alumni, teachers, and students joined hands and swung into action. Neighborhood activists led strategizing sessions and divvied up responsibilities. Teachers and community allies composed talking points and fact sheets. A few of my students created an animated video that explained how closing the branch would negatively impact kids. A number of us, including many parents, went to speak at Board of Education meetings. We held several after-school rallies to elicit community support.

Of course, none of this made Quincy any different from the many other schools whose buildings had been threatened with closure over the years. No community just sat back, arms folded, and waited for it to happen. People resisted. In Chicago's forgotten neighborhoods, schools are often steadying forces. Even when they may not be judged successful by the metrics set by CPS, they are still home to the accomplishments of generations past and the aspirations of those to come. As Eve Ewing puts it in *Ghosts in the Schoolyard,*[3] her book about the impact of school closings on the historically Black community of Bronzeville:

> The people of Bronzeville understand that a school is more than a school. A school is a site of history and a pillar of pride in a racist city. A school is a safe place to be. A school is a place where you find a family. A school is a home. So when they come for your schools, they're coming for you.[4]

For the students I teach, and their families, that is not an unfamiliar feeling. *They're coming for us.* CPS was but another encroaching foe to add to the list: the occupant of the White House, ICE agents, stray bullets from the other side. *They're coming for us.* Sometimes, in the heat of a classroom moment, I catch myself telling a kid who seems to be drifting, "Hey, come on—focus! You need to focus!" Later, when I'm able to put things into better perspective, I wonder: How would I ever focus if I were in their shoes?

As I write this, 2 years after we were first notified about plans to close Quincy's branch building, the talk of doing so has quieted. Whether our protests and counterarguments made a difference or the

Board of Education has been too busy with other priorities is hard to know. But for now, we are okay.

For now.

* * *

A framed 8 × 10 photo of Leo, taken just weeks before he was killed, is still on display atop a bookcase in my classroom, directly behind where he used to sit. In it, he is grinning, wearing a Seattle Seahawks jersey, his dark hair swooping down across his forehead. My class still meditates daily, and often, when the chime sounds, I'm briefly taken back to that unbearably difficult time. I think about Leo's family. I wonder about his classmates. I remember him in silence.

In the two and a half years since he was killed, gun violence in the community has calmed somewhat. Fewer altars adorn the sidewalks. When asked, kids talk about it with relief, but many also seem to be holding their breath, worried that the peace could be shattered in an instant, that another shooting could happen any day.

I hope not. But they are not unwise to worry. City leaders have done little to address the underlying causes of gun violence in Chicago's impoverished communities. If you ask the young men in our Reflections group what's needed—older teens and twenty-somethings who are struggling—their answers form a singular refrain: "We don't need more police. We need jobs."

It may sound like a simplistic response, but as Myles Horton said of his work with poor and working families in Appalachia, the people with the problems are the people with the solutions. A similar notion formed the basis of the earliest efforts at community organizing in Back of the Yards. In the late 1930s, the Back of the Yards Neighborhood Council was established with the motto, "We the people will work out our own destiny."[5] That spirit continues today. When I ask Ismael, one of my current 7th graders, what he appreciates most about the community, he says, "Even though things are hard, people here keep trying to make the neighborhood better. There's bad things, but year after year, people keep trying to create more good things, too."

Many of the people creating those good things are young: in their twenties and thirties. They are grassroots activists and entrepreneurs, students and professionals, dreamers and doers—all committed to finding new ways to represent, uplift, and further beautify the neighborhood. Jesse Iniguez and Mayra Hernandez used crowd funding to open the neighborhood's first and only coffee shop, which hosts arts and storytelling events and employs young people from the area. Hugo Dominguez, an undocumented college student from Mexico, joined with Back of the Yards natives Jose Alonso and Yazmin Velazquez to start Dreamers and Allies Run, a volunteer-led effort that has raised over $80,000 for scholarships for undocumented students. Mayra Lopez-Zuñiga has helped make Back of the Yards a nexus of political engagement on the southwest side by leading several successful political campaigns for progressive local candidates. Rolando Santoyo created a product line, La Selva Shop, which promotes pride in the hood through fashion and design. Claudia Alvidrez and three friends formed Amor al Arte, which provides free art experiences to local youth and "pop-up" public art projects during the summer months. Berto Aguayo, a gang member during his younger days, is a youth organizer and founder of the Increase the Peace initiative, which hosts all-night campouts for young people as a visible counter to street violence. So much inspiring, essential work.

Over the last few years, I have invited a number of these young adults, many of whom once attended Quincy, to come speak with my students and share their stories. When you're in 7th or 8th grade, your dreams can seem far away, even if you are a kid whose family is flush with resources, whose language and skin color mark you as unmistakably American. When daily life is more of a struggle—when the rent is overdue, when you are undocumented, when a parent gets laid off, when a cop harasses you for no reason, when you are Black or brown or Muslim or trans or gay, when you can't imagine how you'd ever get the money to pay for college—dreams can seem even more distant and unreachable. They can seem like wishes, not ambitions. But meeting a person who once had similar dreams, who was raised in the same place as you, went to the same school, sat in the same seat—that can bring a shift in perspective.

The connecting thread in all the discussions with these classroom guests was not financial success or crowning accomplishments. Instead, the common themes related to overcoming challenges, love for the community, and engaging in work that impacts others in a positive way. I can, and do, talk with my students about these same things. But hearing it from me is different than hearing it from someone who has walked in your shoes. For my kids, these young community leaders serve as living, breathing mirrors—conduits to conjuring a vision of their possible future selves.

* * *

On parent–teacher conference day, in a crowded gymnasium, I sit across a small table from one of my homeroom students, Gabriela, and her mom. Gabriela seems a bit nervous, as kids often are before a conference. Her mom's eyes look tired. Under normal circumstances, I would refer to the mother as "Ms. Chacon," but instead I call her by her first name—Oralia. I have a good reason to. I've known her for 20 years—since 1998, when she, too, was a student of mine at Quincy. Now she's here to check on her daughter's progress. The circle completes.

I tell Oralia how bright her daughter is. A phenomenal writer. A deep thinker. Insightful during class discussions. Attuned to issues of equity. Helps other students feel included. Gabriela shrinks a bit under all the compliments, but I can tell she is also proud, happy for her mother to hear all this coming from me.

"I know," Oralia says. "I tell her all the time. She's so smart, so talented."

I ask Gabriela if she'd like to show her mom the Identity Collage video she made—an assignment from our media class. She flashes a bashful smile and looks away, but says yes. In the short video, Gabriela talks about having only a mother growing up; not having a sibling until she was 7; how much her family means to her. The visuals are all family photos—many of them shots of Gabriela and Oralia together through the years. Their bond, it's clear, is strong.

When the video ends, I look up from the iPad to see tears flowing down Oralia's face. I probably should have expected it, but somehow I am caught by surprise. My eyes begin to sting. I have the urge to break the silence, but no words come, so I just soak everything in.

"I'm so proud of her," Oralia says, still wiping away tears. "I wasn't a very good student. School was hard for me. But she is doing so good. And I just keep pushing her, keep telling her—you can do it." She turns to Gabriela. "You can achieve so many things I wasn't able to do."

There are days as a teacher when it seems the world is unspooling beneath your feet. There are days, too, marked by tedium and routine. But there are also moments—not entire days, but moments—that are almost spiritual. They are not usually things you anticipate or plan, but moments you are simply grateful to be part of, to bear witness to. And it is in such moments, though too few and far between, that I am reminded most clearly of why I returned to the classroom.

There are also still moments when I feel disheartened, adrift in the absurdity of what public education has become. Sure, I try to make my classroom a refuge from the test-and-punish, scores-and-ratings, all-about-the-numbers madness, but it's not a leak-proof shelter. When opportunities are offered to, or withheld from, your students based largely on how they perform on standardized tests, you can't just ignore them. At least I can't. The danger is that, little by little, the system changes you more than you change it. Then one day you look at yourself in the mirror and realize you're not the teacher you want to be or even the one you used to be. So far, I still recognize myself—on the days I even have time to glance in a mirror.

One afternoon after a particularly draining day, I ask a class of my 7th graders, "What advice would you give to someone who is thinking about becoming a teacher?"

"Don't do it!" someone shouts out immediately, and laughter fills the room. Ask a group of teachers the same question these days, and a number of them would probably give a similar response. It's understandable. It's a difficult time to be a teacher. But the truth is that teaching has never been easy. Doing it well is even harder.

On Twitter one evening, I pause on a tweet that consists of only two words—"Why teach?"—alongside a photo of a page from a book. A single paragraph is highlighted. Curious, I tap the photo to enlarge it and, as I begin to read, I immediately recognize the words. They are mine—from the final pages of *Holler If You Hear Me*,[6] my memoir of my early years as a teacher, first published in 1999:

> At the core of our work [as teachers] is the belief, despite the distressing signs around us, that the world is indeed changeable, that it can be made into a better, more just, more peaceful place, and that the kids who show up in our classrooms each day not only deserve such a world, but can be instrumental in helping to bring it about. Their voices are abiding reminders that there is something to hope for in spite of the hopelessness that seems to be closing in around us—something tangible, something real, something in the here and now.[7]

It's the first time I've reread those words in years, and it is odd, not to mention surprising, to see them staring back at me in a tweet. The critic in me thinks they sound too flowery and idealistic. But a more generous part of me is struck by how much they still resonate all these years later. Sure, a lot has changed in schools and in the world outside them. But the core of what I believe about teaching, and why I teach, remains constant: All kids—especially those our public schools have too often failed throughout this nation's history—deserve an education that honors and validates who they are, that makes room for their questions and concerns, that challenges them to think deeply, that engages their creative spirit, that helps them find meaning in a sometimes hostile and confusing world.

Nearly 30 years after starting out as a teacher in Chicago, the daily reality in my classroom still falls short of that vision too much of the time. But as frustrating as that can be, I haven't wavered in my commitment to reach toward it. I am reminded of a scene from what is still one of my favorite pieces of fiction to read with students—Sandra Cisneros's *The House on Mango Street*—when young Esperanza looks out her apartment window and, amid the concrete landscape, sees four skinny trees. Four trees, Cisneros writes, "who reach and do not forget to reach."[8]

Not a bad rule of thumb for a teacher.

Notes

Chapter 2

1. Flanders, 2012.
2. Chicago Tribune Editorial Board, 2012.
3. Peterson, 1997.
4. Ibid.
5. Muskal, 2012.
6. PBS News Hour, 2012.
7. Ashby & Bruno, 2016, p. 2.
8. G1 & RodStarz, 2012.

Chapter 3

1. CBS Evening News, 2012.
2. Christensen, 2000.
3. Horn, 2012.
4. Coates, 2015, p. 26.
5. Ayers & Alexander-Tanner, 2010, p. 24.

Chapter 4

1. Netter et al. & Lee, 2012.

Chapter 5

1. City of Chicago, 2013.
2. Democracy Now, 2013.
3. Atwell, 2007.
4. Miller, 2009.
5. Atwell, 2007.
6. Miller, 2009, p. 34.

Chapter 6

1. McIntosh & Style, 1999.
2. Sims Bishop, 1990.
3. Sullivan, 2014.
4. Ibid.
5. Moore, 2015.
6. Nazaryan, 2012.
7. Ibid.
8. Myers, 1986.
9. Caref et al., 2012.
10. Cooperative Children's Book Center, 2018.
11. Educolor, 2018.
12. Tatum, 2003.
13. U.S. Department of Education, 2016.
14. For more, see americanindiansinchildrensliterature.blogspot.com/p/best-books.html.
15. For more, see diversebooks.org.
16. For more, see disrupttexts.org/lets-get-to-work.
17. For more, see Valeria Brown's #ClearTheAir website at cleartheaireducation.wordpress.com.
18. Adichie, 2009.
19. Ibid.

Chapter 7

1. Hagopian, 2014, p. 15.
2. Brackett, 2014.
3. Karp, 2014.
4. Madhani, 2017.

Chapter 8

1. Sara Ahmed would like to acknowledge Harvey "Smokey" Daniels and James Beane as the original inspirations for this phrase.
2. For an in-depth, thoughtful discussion on this, see Matthew Kay's book, *Not Light, But Fire: How to Lead Meaningful Race Conversations in the Classroom.*
3. For more, see Marcia Chatelain's article in The Atlantic about why she started #FergusonSyllabus: https://www.theatlantic.com/education

/archive/2014/08/how-to-teach-kids-about-whats-happening-in-ferguson /379049/.

4. Police State USA, 2014.
5. Zinn, 2005.
6. United States Department of Justice, 2015.
7. Horwitz, 2015.
8. Kay, 2018.
9. Ibid., pp. 242–243.
10. Ibid., p. 242.

Chapter 9

1. Kohl, 2003.
2. Ibid., p. 4.
3. American Statistical Association, 2014.
4. Illinois Association of School Boards, 2018.

Chapter 10

1. ABC News, 2016.
2. Thompson, 2019, personal communication.

Chapter 11

1. Borger, 2017.

Chapter 12

1. Petrella, 2017.
2. Hauser, 2016.
3. Legal Information Institute, n.d.
4. Chicago Teachers Union, n.d.
5. Shalaby, 2017.

Chapter 13

1. Klein, 2017.
2. Simon, 1997.
3. Ibid.
4. Ibid.
5. GLSEN, 2017.

Chapter 14

1. Picker & Sun, 2013.

2. From an advertisement for "Southern Mob Rule," a lecture by Ida B. Wells, *Washington Bee*, October 22, 1892.

3. This quote consists of several of Mariame Kaba's tweets combined into a single narrative.

4. Mohan, 2018.

5. Freire, 1998.

6. Ibid., pp. 39–40.

Chapter 15

1. Minor, 2019.
2. Rothstein, 2017.
3. Ewing, 2018.
4. Ibid., pp. 155–156.
5. Slayton, 2004.
6. Michie, 2009.
7. Ibid., p. 193.
8. Cisneros, 1989, p. 75.

References

ABC News. (2016, August 1). *Full text: Khizr Khan's speech to the 2016 Democratic National Convention*. Retrieved from abcnews.go.com/Politics/full-text-khizr-khans-speech-2016-democratic-national/story?id=41043609

Adichie, C. N. (2009). *The danger of a single story* [Video file]. Retrieved from www.ted.com/talks/chimamanda_adichie_the_danger_of_a_single_story/up-next

American Statistical Association (ASA). (2014). *ASA statement on using value-added models for educational assessment (Executive Summary)*. Retrieved from www.scribd.com/document/217916454/ASA-VAM-Statement-1

Ashby, S. K., & Bruno, R. (2016). *A fight for the soul of public education: The story of the Chicago teachers strike*. Ithaca, NY: ILR Press.

Atwell, N. (2007). *The reading zone: How to help kids become skilled, passionate, habitual, critical readers*. New York, NY: Scholastic.

Ayers, W., & Alexander-Tanner, R. (2010). *To teach: The journey, in comics*. New York, NY: Teachers College Press.

Borger, J. (2017, May 3). Rex Tillerson: 'America first' means divorcing our policy from our values. *The Guardian*. Retrieved from www.theguardian.com/us-news/2017/may/03/rex-tillerson-america-first-speech-trump-policy

Brackett, E. (2014, February 26). Some CPS teachers boycotting ISAT. *WTTW*. Retrieved from news.wttw.com/2014/02/26/some-cps-teachers-boycotting-isat

Caref, C., Hainds, S., Hilgendorf, K., Jankov, K., & Russell, P. (2012). *The black and white of education in Chicago's public schools: Class, charters, and chaos*. Chicago Teachers Union. Retrieved from www.ctulocal1

.org/wp-content/uploads/2018/10/CTU-black-and-white-of-chicago-education.pdf

CBS Evening News. (2012, July 10). *Emanuel: Chicago's escalating crime about 'values.'* Retrieved from www.cbsnews.com/news/emanuel-chicagos-escalating-crime-about-values

Chicago Teachers Union (n.d.). *Professional personnel leadership committees.* Retrieved from www.ctulocal1.org/movement/tools/pplc

Chicago Tribune Editorial Board. (2012, September 11). Don't cave, Mr. Mayor. *Chicago Tribune.* Retrieved from www.chicagotribune.com/opinion/ct-xpm-2012-09-11-ct-edit-strike-0911-jm-20120911-story.html

Christensen, L. (2000). *Reading, writing, and rising up: Teaching about social justice and the power of the written word.* Milwaukee, WI: Rethinking Schools.

Cisneros, S. (1989). *The house on Mango Street.* New York, NY: Vintage Books.

City of Chicago. (2013, March 26). *Mayor Emanuel and CPS CEO Barbara Byrd-Bennett announce up to 50 Learning Gardens will be installed in welcoming schools this fall.* Retrieved from www.chicago.gov/city/en/depts/mayor/press_room/press_releases/2013/march_2013/mayor_emanuel_andcpsceobarbarabyrd-bennettannounceupto50learning.html

Coates, T. (2015). *Between the world and me.* New York, NY: Spiegel & Grau.

Cooperative Children's Book Center. (2018). *Publishing statistics on children's books about people of color and first/native nations.* Retrieved from ccbc.education.wisc.edu/books/pcstats.asp#charts

Democracy Now. (2013, May 28). *Chicago to shutter 50 public schools: Is historic mass closure an experiment in privatization?* Retrieved from www.democracynow.org/2013/5/28/chicago_to_shutter_50_public_schools

Educolor. (2018). *Educolor chats.* Retrieved from www.educolor.org/category/educolor-chat

Ewing, E. (2018). *Ghosts in the schoolyard: Racism and school closings on Chicago's south side.* Chicago, IL: University of Chicago Press.

Flanders, L. (2012, September 10). Why strike? Hear it from a Chicago teacher. *The Nation.* Retrieved from www.thenation.com/article/why-strike-hear-it-chicago-teacher-video

Freire, P. (1985). *The politics of education: Culture, power, and liberation.* Westport, CT: Bergin & Garvey.

Freire, P. (1998). *Teachers as cultural workers: Letters to those who dare teach.* Boulder, CO: Westview Press.

G1 & RodStarz. (2012). Chicago teacher. [Recorded by Rebel Diaz]. Available at rebeldiaz.bandcamp.com/track/chicago-teacher

GLSEN. (2017). *The 2016 National School Climate Survey: Executive Summary.* Retrieved from www.glsen.org/sites/default/files/GLSEN%202017%20 National%20School%20Climate%20Survey%20%28NSCS%29%20 -%20Executive%20Summary%20%28English%29.pdf

Hagopian, J. (2014). *More than a score: The new uprising against high-stakes testing.* Chicago, IL: Haymarket Books.

Hauser, C. (2016, August 27). Why Colin Kaepernick didn't stand for the National Anthem. *New York Times.* Retrieved from www.nytimes.com /2016/08/28/sports/football/colin-kaepernick-national-anthem-49ers -stand.html

Horn, J. (2012, April 29). David Coleman's global revenge and the Common Core [Blog post]. Retrieved from www.schoolsmatter.info/2012/04 /david-colemans-global-revenge-and.html

Horwitz, S. (2015, March 4). Justice department clears Ferguson police officer in civil rights probe. *Washington Post.* Retrieved from www.washington post.com/world/national-security/justice-dept-review-finds-pattern-of -racial-bias-among-ferguson-police/2015/03/03/27535390-c1c7-11e4 -9271-610273846239_story.html?utm_term=.88404a029f69

Illinois Association of School Boards. (2018). *PERA overview for school board members.* Retrieved from www.iasb.com/law/PERAoverview.pdf

Karp, S. (2014, March 1). More teachers to boycott ISAT, as parents rally behind them. *Chicago Reporter.* Retrieved from www.chicagoreporter .com/more-teachers-boycott-isat-parents-rally-behind-them

Kay, M. R. (2018). *Not light, but fire: How to lead meaningful race conversations in the classroom.* Portsmouth, NH: Stenhouse.

Klein, A. (2017, December 12). Survey: Educators' political leanings, who they voted for, where they stand on key issues. *Education Week.* Retrieved from www.edweek.org/ew/articles/2017/12/13/survey-paints -political-portrait-of-americas-k-12.html

Kohl, H. (2003). *Stupidity and tears: Teaching and learning in troubled times.* New York, NY: The New Press.

Legal Information Institute (n.d.). *West Virginia State Board of Education v. Barnette.* Retrieved from www.law.cornell.edu/supremecourt/text /319/624

Madhani, A. (2017, April 28). Ex-Chicago schools chief gets 4 1/2 years in prison for bribery scheme. *USA Today.* Retrieved from www.usatoday.com/story/news/2017/04/28/ex-chicago-schools-chief-faces-sentencing-kickback-scheme/101021272

McIntosh, P., & Style, E. (1999). Social, emotional, and political learning. In J. Cohen (Ed.), *Educating minds and hearts: Social emotional learning and the passage into adolescence* (pp. 137–157). New York, NY: Teachers College Press.

Michie, G. (2009). *Holler if you hear me: The education of a teacher and his students* (2nd ed.). New York, NY: Teachers College Press.

Miller, D. (2009). *The book whisperer: Awakening the inner reader in every child.* San Francisco, CA: Jossey-Bass.

Minor, C. (2019). *We got this: Equity, access, and the quest to be who our students need us to be.* Portsmouth, NH: Heinemann.

Mohan, P. (2018, August 8). How these women raised $42K in a day for an Ida B. Wells monument. *Fast Company.* Retrieved from www.fastcompany.com/90211495/how-these-women-raised-42k-in-a-day-for-a-ida-b-wells-monument

Moore, N. (2015, July 14). Why are there fewer black teachers in CPS? *WBEZ.* Retrieved from www.wbez.org/shows/wbez-news/why-are-there-fewer-black-teachers-in-cps/06514798-d677-4235-ad5c-4a977700e2cb

Muskal, M. (2012, September 12). Chicago teachers strike enters 3rd day; 'long strike' warned. *Los Angeles Times.* Retrieved from articles.latimes.com/2012/sep/12/nation/la-na-nn-chicago-teachers-strike-20120912

Myers, W. D. (1986, November 9). 'I thought we would revolutionize the industry.' *New York Times.* Retrieved from www.nytimes.com/1986/11/09/books/children-s-books-i-actually-thought-we-would-revolutionize-the-industry.html

Nazaryan, A. (2012, January 4). Against Walter Dean Myers and the dumbing down of literature: 'Those kids' can read Homer. *Daily News.* Retrieved from www.nydailynews.com/blogs/pageviews/walter-dean-myers-dumbing-literature-kids-read-homer-blog-entry-1.1637371

Netter, G., et al. (Producers), & Lee, A. (Director). (2012). *Life of Pi* [Motion picture]. United States: Fox 2000 Pictures.

PBS News Hour. (2012, September 19). *Students of Chicago public schools back in class, broader reform issues remain.* Retrieved from www.pbs.org/newshour/show/chicago-schools-back-in-session-reform-issues-remain#transcript

Peterson, B. (1997). We need a new vision of teacher unionism. *Rethinking Schools, 11*(4). Retrieved from rethinkingschools.aidcvt.com/special_reports/union/un11_4.shtml

Petrella, C. (2017, November 3). The ugly history of the Pledge of Allegiance—and why it matters. *Washington Post.* Retrieved from www.washingtonpost.com/news/made-by-history/wp/2017/11/03/the-ugly-history-of-the-pledge-of-allegiance-and-why-it-matters/?utm_term=.0a55c370bda0

Picker, M., & Sun, C. (Producers), & Picker, M., & Sun, C. (Directors). (2013). *Latinos beyond reel: Challenging a media stereotype* [Motion picture]. United States: Media Education Foundation.

Police State USA. (2014, August 16). *Missouri Jay Nixon declares state of emergency, mandatory curfew in Ferguson* [Video file]. Retrieved from www.youtube.com/watch?time_continue=120&v=2zspevpRgEU

Rothstein, R. (2017). *The color of law: A forgotten history of how our government segregated America.* New York: Liveright Publishing.

Shalaby, C. (2017). *Troublemakers: Lessons in freedom from young children at school.* New York, NY: The New Press.

Simon, L. A. (Director). (1997). *Fear and learning at Hoover Elementary* [Motion picture]. United States: Tracy Trench Productions.

Sims Bishop, R. (1990). Mirrors, windows, and sliding glass doors. *Perspectives, 1*(3), ix–xi.

Slayton, R. (2004). Back of the Yards Neighborhood Council. *Encyclopedia of Chicago.* Retrieved from www.encyclopedia.chicagohistory.org/pages/100.html

Sullivan, G. (2014, June 26). Student: My school district hires too many white teachers. *Washington Post.* Retrieved from www.washingtonpost.com/posteverything/wp/2014/06/26/my-school-district-hires-too-many-white-teachers/?utm_term=.3543a9389906

Tatum, B. D. (2003). *"Why are all the Black kids sitting together in the cafeteria?" And other conversations about race.* New York, NY: Basic Books.

United States Department of Education. (2016, July). *The state of racial diversity in the educator workforce.* Retrieved from www2.ed.gov/rschstat/eval/highered/racial-diversity/state-racial-diversity-workforce.pdf.

United States Department of Justice. (2015, March 24). *Justice Department announces findings of two civil rights investigations in Ferguson, Missouri.* Retrieved from www.justice.gov/opa/pr/justice-department

-announces-findings-two-civil-rights-investigations-ferguson-missouri

Zinn, H. (2005, April 27). "To be neutral, to be passive in a situation is to collaborate with whatever is going on." (A. Goodman, interviewer). *Democracy Now*. Retrieved from www.democracynow.org/2005/4/27/howard_zinn_to_be_neutral_to

About the Author

Gregory Michie teaches 7th and 8th graders in Chicago's Back of the Yards neighborhood. He taught in Chicago public schools from 1990 until 1999, when he left to pursue a PhD in education. He spent a decade as an education professor at three universities, working primarily with preservice and novice teachers in Chicago. In 2012, he returned to classroom teaching. He is the author of *Holler If You Hear Me: The Education of a Teacher and His Students* (2nd edition, 2009), *See You When We Get There: Teaching for Change in Urban Schools* (2005), *We Don't Need Another Hero: Struggle, Hope, and Possibility in the Age of High-Stakes Schooling* (2012), all from Teachers College Press. He is currently collaborating with Ryan Alexander-Tanner and 10 young artists to create a comic edition of *Holler If You Hear Me* for its 20th anniversary.